Action Research for Improving Practice

A Practical Guide

Action Research for Improving Practice

A Practical Guide

Valsa Koshy

Paul Chapman Publishing

London · Thousand Oaks · New Delhi

First published 2005

Paul Chapman Publishing
A SAGE Publications Company
1 Oliver's Yard
55 City Road
London EC1Y 1SP

SAGE Publications Inc
2455 Teller Road
Thousand Oaks, California 91320

SAGE Publications India Pvt Ltd
B-42 Panchsheel Enclave
New Delhi 110 017

Library of Congress Control Number 2004117261

A catalogue record for this book is available from the British Library

ISBN 1-4129-0755-1
ISBN 1-4129-0756-X (pbk)

Typeset by Pantek Arts Ltd, Maidstone, Kent
Printed in Great Britain by TJ International Ltd, Padstow Cornwall

Contents

Acknowledgements

I am indebted to many people and organisations for providing me with the opportunity to support practitioners with their action research. I have learnt a great deal from these experiences and this learning has guided me in writing this book. Although it is impossible for me to list all the people who have influenced me over the years, I would like to express my thanks to all of them. My special thanks to the following:

- The Department for Education and Skills (DfES) for providing funding to enable 14 research partners, across the country, to research into aspects of a complex and challenging topic – developing gifts and talents of children aged 5–7. I had the privilege of experiencing the impact of the action research process on their own practice and the enhancement of opportunities for the children. This opportunity convinced me of the significant role of practitioner research for improving practice.

- All the practitioners and students I have guided, over the years, to carry out action research at undergraduate and postgraduate levels and those who carried out action research for funded projects from the Teaching Training Agency and local education authorities. I shared the level of enthusiasm, excitement and commitment of these people and learnt a great deal from these experiences.

- The many children I have observed, who were the ultimate beneficiaries of the action research carried out by the practitioners.

Finally, I dedicate this book to my husband Ron Casey, who is the most influential tutor I have had throughout my academic career. Discussing educational issues with him and listening to him continually questioning and challenging perspectives often highlighted the need for practitioners to reflect on their practices so as to initiate changes with increased understanding and confidence.

Introduction

Doing a piece of research on how to enhance the learning opportunities of gifted children has been the most rewarding experience of my working life. I secured a grant from the Teacher Training Agency which enabled me to use action research to design a lens to get my classroom work into focus – magnifying what was good and gratifying, but also highlighting those aspects in need of redirection and rejuvenation. Before that elevating experience I assumed that all forms of research were the exclusive province of academic researchers in universities. Gaining access to that ivory tower has enabled one practitioner – me – to illuminate sound strategies to enable colleagues to navigate their way through the parts of the maze of gifted education.

Laura, a classroom teacher (1997)

I vividly remember Laura's excitement when she secured a grant from the Teacher Training Agency to carry out a piece of action research on a topic relating to provision for very able pupils, which I had the privilege of supervising. At the time of obtaining the grant there had been very little research carried out on aspects of provision for higher ability pupils in England and Wales. Laura's interest stemmed from her noticing how bored some children were in her classroom. A recent comment from an inspection report by the Office for Standards in Education (OFSTED) that the whole school needed to address the issue of more effective provision for very able children confirmed her reason for concern. She carried out the study within ten months, in stages: defining the topic for her research, finding out what was happening in her class and that of a willing colleague, reading around the topic, planning activities which demanded higher cognitive skills, collecting and analyzing data, and evaluating and disseminating her findings to her colleagues at her school and at the local teachers' centre. She also sent a final report to the Teacher Training Agency in the form of a case study. My aim in writing this book is to share some of my experiences, such as supervising Laura's action research, and to generate a set of guidelines for practitioners to enable them to undertake action research so as to enhance their own professional practice as well as to provide leadership to their colleagues.

Similar testimonies to that of Laura's, from practitioners, on the benefits of undertaking action research were reported in a recent special issue of the *Times Education Supplement* (2004), appropriately titled *Classroom Discoveries*. In it, MacGarvey compares teacher researchers to gardeners nurturing new plants and shares her experience of working with teachers who are enthusiastic about practitioner research, are keen to test out theories about learning styles and motivational strategies and are interested in methods of investigation. Chan (TES, 2004: 9), a head of English in a school, describes classroom research as a learning process. She maintains:

> Using a research model allows us to trust our conclusions, like any scientific 'fair test'. When I have examined the problem, done my background reading, found out possibilities that I had not thought of before, chosen my methodology and come to new conclusions for dealing with the issues – then I feel positive about myself as a professional. But even if I cannot sort out a problem, I can at least talk knowledgeably about the issues involved …

In the past few years, action research has become increasingly popular as a mode of research among practitioners. The main role of action research is to facilitate practitioners to study aspects of practice – whether it is in the context of introducing an innovative idea or in assessing and reflecting on the effectiveness of existing practice, with the view of improving practice. This process is often carried out within the researcher's own setting. The importance of professional development for enhancing the quality of practice has long been recognised both within the United Kingdom and abroad. Hargreaves (1996) points out that research-based practice would be more effective and satisfying for practitioners. The commitment of the government was clearly stated in the Department for Education and Employment (DfEE) document (2001) *Learning and Teaching: A Strategy for Professional Development*. As part of the Continuing Professional Development programme, the Department for Education and Skills (DfES) has been providing funding – described as *best practice* awards – to enable teachers and other professionals to carry out small-scale research projects on various aspects of education. Reports of these projects are often published on the DfES website as case studies for others to share. Other agencies also offer opportunities for practising teachers to undertake action research projects. More information on these can be found at the end of this book.

Action research is, quite often, the method of enquiry employed by undergraduate and postgraduate students in higher education who are studying for accredited courses. In recent years, students studying for taught doctorate (EdD) degrees with their focus on practical aspects of education are also adopting action research as a method of study. This book attempts to meet the needs of all the above groups of people by providing a coherent, accessible and practical set of guidelines on how to carry out action research.

The contents of this book draw on my personal experience of 15 years in guiding researchers in various settings – as Course Leader for Masters programmes, as Director of Academic and Professional Development and also through my involvement in research training for doctoral students at my university. During this time I have also supervised a number of practising teachers carrying out funded action research projects. Recently, I have been commissioned by the DfES to lead a group of 14 research partners – practitioners – to carry out small-scale projects relating to the nurturing and development of talent in children aged 4 to 7 years. All these experiences have enabled me to question and refine my own understanding of action research as a process.

As the main purpose of this book is to offer practical guidance to those who intend to carry out action research, I feel it is important to ask three questions:

- What is action research?

- When would it be appropriate for a practitioner to carry out action research?

- How would one go about carrying out action research?

I have attempted to address all three questions in this book. To start us on the right track, it would be useful to consider why we may undertake action research. Doing action research facilitates evaluation and reflection in order to implement necessary changes in practice – both for an individual and within an institution – with increased understanding and confidence. As new initiatives are introduced with greater frequency, practitioners can often be left with conflicting viewpoints, doubts and dilemmas which need exploration, evaluation and reflection. Evaluating one's own practices is an integral part of an applied discipline such as education.

This book addresses the needs of two groups of researchers:

- Those who wish to undertake small-scale research into an aspect of their practice. This may be facilitated by external funding or may be the outcome of a local necessity to evaluate the effectiveness of an innovation or an initiative. The processes involved in undertaking an action research project would involve looking at issues in depth and gathering and assessing the evidence before implementing new ideas or changing one's practices.

- Students – undergraduate, postgraduate or those studying for practical doctorate courses – who wish to carry out research as part of accredited courses. Some of the projects within this context may, of course, belong to the first category when a university course may provide added support to the action researcher.

I hope that both the above groups will find the step-by-step guidance provided in this book useful.

My own belief is that carrying out action research is all about developing the act of knowing through observation, listening, analysing, questioning and being involved in constructing one's own knowledge. The new knowledge and experiences inform the researcher's future direction and influences action.

This book is written in an interactive style and the reader is invited to join the author in exploring aspects of what is involved in conducting *practitioner research* as it is sometimes called. The use of examples and case studies throughout the book should make the contents accessible.

The book is presented in seven chapters. **Chapter 1** will explore the concept of action research and consider how it is distinctive from other forms of research. Readers will be provided with an overview of how action research has developed over the past decades, its background and the key concepts of action research – planning action, evaluation, refinement, reflection, theory building. References to experts' views and models on action research should assist the new action researcher to plan his or her work as well as help to justify the choice. Possible advantages of using action research as a methodology are discussed here. Detailed examples of action research projects, carried out by practitioners from a variety of contexts and dealing with a range of topics, are presented in this chapter.

Chapters 2 to 6 will address the various stages of action research. In *Chapter 2*, I will address some of the criticisms raised against action research as a methodology. It will explore some definitions of action research offered by experts and discuss the structure and processes involved in conducting action research. The aim of this chapter is to offer practical guidelines to action researchers who are about to take the first step. It offers examples of topics selected by practitioners for action research. Although the stages of action research are not strictly linear, it should help the researcher to think in terms of planning the project in stages – with built-in flexibility to refine, make adjustments and change direction within the structure. This feature of flexibility for refinement makes action research an eminently suitable method of enquiry for practitioners. Using examples, the reader is guided in his or her choice of topic for research, as well as helping them to consider the suitability of using action research in various contexts.

Chapter 3 focuses on the role of literature search and writing research reviews within action research. The justification for undertaking research reviews and guidance on how to gather, organise, analyse and make use of what is read, are presented in this chapter.

Having selected a topic and collected background literature, the researcher would then be planning the project. *Chapter 4* supports the reader, using practical examples to illustrate how interventions and activities have been planned by other practitioners. In my experience, one of the most challenging aspects of conducting action research is in making decisions on what kind of data is needed and how to collect it to achieve the aims of the project. In *Chapter 5*, different types of instrumentation for gathering data are presented. Using practical illustrations, the advantages and disadvantages of using different methods are discussed. The importance of being systematic in the data-gathering process is emphasised.

Chapter 6 focuses on the complex issue of the analysis of data and data display. Action research, by its nature, is unlikely to produce universally generalisable findings – its purpose is to generate principles based on experience. The analysis within action research seeks to identify themes and issues which are relevant and applicable to a particular situation. Guidance is provided on how the data may be analysed and presented. Examples of practitioners' accounts of data analysis are provided within the chapter.

The type of report written by the action researcher will depend on the circumstances of the researcher. Funded research requires a certain format to be followed, whereas a report in the form of a dissertation for an accredited course will need to follow a different and often set format. Examples of writing reports and the processes involved in writing or disseminating findings will be provided in *Chapter 7*.

The reference section in the final part of the book draws on a range of authors who have contributed to the ongoing dialogue on action research. Useful websites, included here, should be helpful for those who wish to undertake action research or are in the process of considering undertaking new research.

What I have attempted in this book is to provide the reader with a clear set of practical guidelines for undertaking action research. I hope you will find them useful. Working alongside action researchers in various settings has provided me with a great deal of enjoyment and satisfaction over the past years. I hope you will share some of what I have experienced, through your reading of this book.

Chapter 1

What is action research?

KEY POINTS

This chapter focuses on:

- the nature of action research;
- the development of action research;
- models of action research proposed by experts in the field;
- examples of action research carried out by practitioners.

INTRODUCTION

During my first meeting with teachers and trainee teachers who are about to undertake action research, I share with them a strong belief I hold. Here it is. I believe that ultimately the quality of educational experiences provided to children will depend on the ability of the teacher to stand back, question and reflect on his or her practice, and continually strive to make the necessary changes. This is true of any practitioner. These processes of reflection and self-evaluation do not happen by accident and I believe that carrying out action research provides practitioners with an opportunity to be engaged in such processes in a meaningful way. With the above statements in mind, I define action research as an enquiry, undertaken with rigour and understanding so as to constantly refine practice; the emerging evidence-based outcomes will then contribute to the researching practitioner's continuing professional development.

In this chapter I will trace the development of action research as a methodology over the past few decades and then consider the different perspectives and models provided by experts in the field. Different models of action research are explored and an attempt is made to identify the unique features of action research which make it an attractive mode of research for practitioners. An understanding of different interpretations and viewpoints of action research should be useful to readers whether they are about to start a project or are in the process of doing one. Researchers who are carrying out action research as part of an accredited course are usually expected to demonstrate their understanding of the processes involved. Those who are involved in action research following personal interests or as part of a funded project will also need to gain insights into the processes involved, so that they can engage in action research with greater confidence and understanding.

THE DEVELOPMENT OF ACTION RESEARCH: A BRIEF BACKGROUND

Whether you are a novice or are progressing with an action research project, it would be useful for you to be aware of how action research developed as a method for carrying out research over the past few decades. Zeichner (2001) and Hopkins (2002) provide us with an overview of how action research developed as a research tradition. The work of Kurt Lewin (1946), who researched into social issues, is often described as a major landmark in the development of action research as a methodology. Lewin's work was followed by that of Stephen Corey and others in the USA, who applied this methodology for researching into educational issues.

In Britain, according to Hopkins (2002), the origins of action research can be traced back to the Schools Council's Humanities Curriculum Project (1967–72) with its emphasis on an experimental curriculum and the reconceptualisation of curriculum development. Following on this project, Elliot and Adelman (1976) used action research in their Teaching Project, examining classroom practice.

The most well known proponent of action research in the UK has been Lawrence Stenhouse (1975) whose seminal work *An Introduction to Curriculum and Research and Development* added to the appeal of action research for studying the theory and practice of teaching and the curriculum. For Stenhouse (1983), action research was about emancipation and intellectual, moral and spiritual autonomy. There was also the participatory research movement supported by Stephen Kemmis and Robert McTaggart, as reported by Hopkins (2002), at Deakin University in Australia.

In the past two decades action research has been growing in popularity in the United States where it has often been supported by universities. Zeichner (2001) points out that most of the action research carried out in the past involved university academics working with teachers and represented the rejection of a standards or objective-based approach to curriculum development in favour of one that is based on a pedagogy-driven conception of curriculum change as a process dependent on teachers' capacities for reflection. According to this view, Zeichner maintains, the act of curriculum theorising is not so much the application of classroom theory learned in the university as it is the generation of theory from attempts to change curriculum practice in schools.

More recent developments in England and Wales support the important role of action research as reflected in the number of small research grants which have been made available by the Teacher Training Agency and the Department for Education and Skills (DfES) in the past decade. Readers may also be interested to note that the Collaborative Action Research Network (CARN) provides a forum for those interested in action research as a methodology as well as the existence of an international journal, *Educational Action Research*.

WHAT IS INVOLVED IN ACTION RESEARCH?

Research is about generating new knowledge. Action research creates new knowledge based on enquiries conducted within specific and often practical contexts. As articulated earlier, the purpose of action research is to learn through action leading to personal or professional development. It is participatory in nature which led Kemmis and McTaggart

(2000: 595) to describe it as *participatory research*. The authors maintain that action research involves a spiral of self-reflective spirals of:

- planning a change,

- acting and observing the process and consequences of the change,

- reflecting on these processes and consequences and then replanning,

- acting and observing,

- reflecting,

- and so on....

Figure 1.1 **The action research spiral.**

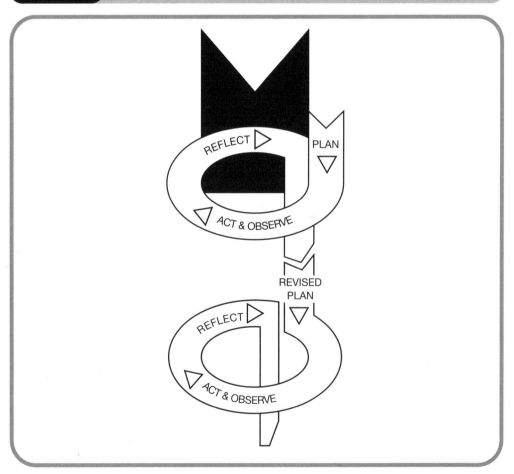

Figure 1.1 illustrates the spiral model of action research proposed by Kemmis and McTaggart, although the authors advise us against using this as a rigid structure. They maintain that in reality the process may not be as neat as the spiral of self-contained cycles of planning, acting and observing, and reflecting suggests. The stages, they maintain, *overlap*, and initial plans quickly become obsolete in the light of learning from experience. *In reality the process is likely to be more fluid, open and responsive.*

I find the spiral model appealing because it offers the opportunity to visit a phenomenon at a higher level each time, and so to progress towards greater overall understanding. By carrying out action research using this model, one can understand a particular issue within an educational context and make informed decisions through enhanced understanding. It is about empowerment.

Several other models have also been put forward by those who have studied different aspects of action research and I will present some of these here. My purpose in so doing is to enable the reader to analyse the principles involved in these models which should, in turn, lead to a deeper understanding of the processes involved in action research. No one specific model is being recommended and, as you may notice, they have many similarities. An action researcher should adopt the models which suit his or her purpose most or adapt them to fit his or her purpose.

The model suggested by Elliot (1991: 71) includes reconnaissance – fact-finding and analysis – within each stage of the action research, as can be seen in Figure 1.2.

Other models, such as O'Leary's (2004: 141) cycles of action research shown in Figure 1.3, portray action research as a cyclic process which takes shape as knowledge emerges.

In O'Leary's model, it is stressed that 'cycles converge towards better situation understanding and improved action implementation; and are based in evaluative practice that alters between action and critical reflection.' (p.140). The author sees action research as an experiential learning approach to change the goal of which is to continually refine the methods, data and interpretation in the light of the understanding developed in the earlier cycles.

Figure 1.2 Elliot's action research model.

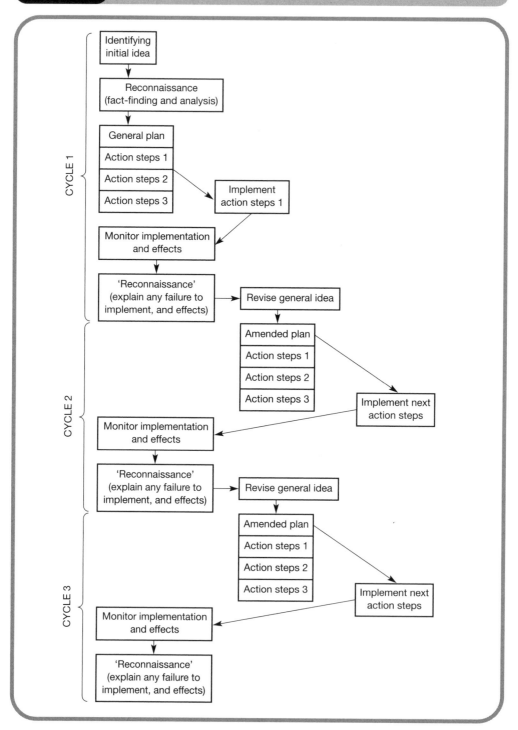

Figure 1.3   O'Leary's cycles of research.

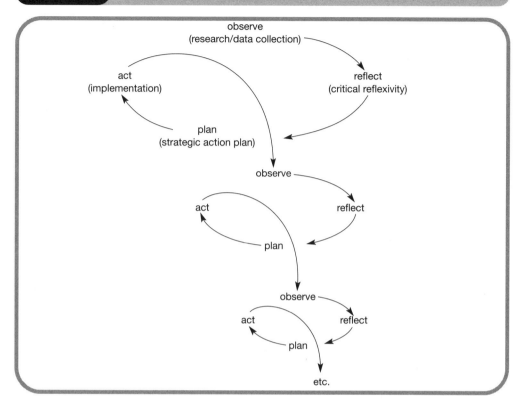

Figure 1.4   An action research cycle.

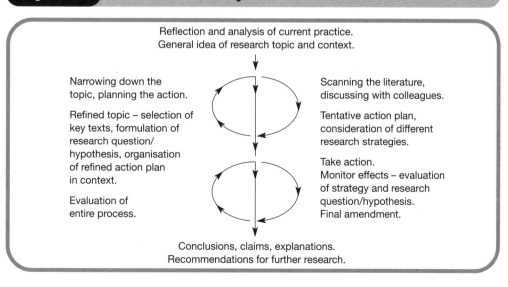

Reflection and analysis of current practice.
General idea of research topic and context.

Narrowing down the
topic, planning the action.

Scanning the literature,
discussing with colleagues.

Refined topic – selection of
key texts, formulation of
research question/
hypothesis, organisation
of refined action plan
in context.

Tentative action plan,
consideration of different
research strategies.

Take action.
Monitor effects – evaluation
of strategy and research
question/hypothesis.
Final amendment.

Evaluation of
entire process.

Conclusions, claims, explanations.
Recommendations for further research.

And finally, in Macintyre's (2000: 1) representation of the stages in action research, the processes involved are signposted as shown in Figure 1.4.

Although it is useful to consider different models, I need to include a word of caution here. Excessive reliance on a particular model, or following the stages or cycles of a particular model too rigidly, could adversely affect the unique opportunity offered by the emerging nature and flexibility which are the hallmarks of action research. Models of practice presented in this chapter are not intended to offer straitjackets to fit an enquiry.

SOME DEFINITIONS OF ACTION RESEARCH

At this point, I feel it may be useful to explore some of the definitions and observations on action research as a methodology offered by different authors. Bassey (1998: 93) describes 'action research as an enquiry which is carried out in order to understand, to evaluate and then to change, in order to improve educational practice'. Hopkins (2002: 41) maintains that 'action research combines a substantive act with a research procedure; it is action disciplined by enquiry, a personal attempt at understanding while engaged in a process of improvement and reform'. Cohen and Manion (1994: 192) describe the emergent nature of action research in their definition. They describe action research as

> essentially an on-the-spot procedure designed to deal with a concrete problem located in an immediate situation. This means that ideally, the step-by-step process is constantly monitored over varying periods of time and by a variety of mechanisms (questionnaires, diaries, interviews and case studies, for example) so that the ensuing feedback may be translated into modifications, adjustment, directional changes, redefinitions, as necessary, so as to bring about lasting benefit to the ongoing process itself rather than to some future occasion.

Bell (1999) comments on the practical, problem-solving nature of action research which she believes makes this approach attractive to practitioner-researchers. She also highlights the fact that action research is directed towards greater understanding and improvement of practice over a period of time. In their introduction to an illuminating collection of papers in the *Handbook of Action Research*, Reason and Bradbury (2001: 2) outline the purpose of action research as the production of practical knowledge that is useful to people in the everyday context of their lives. According to the authors:

> Action research is about working towards practical outcomes, and also about creating new forms of understanding, since action without understanding is blind, just as theory without action is meaningless.

The authors continue to provide valuable insights into the nature of action research:

> Since action research starts with everyday experience and is concerned with the development of living knowledge, in many ways the process of inquiry is as important as specific outcomes. Good action research emerges over time in an evolutionary and developmental process, as individuals develop skills of enquiry and as communities of enquiry develop within communities of practice. (p.2)

A careful study of the definitions and viewpoints I have presented in this section should help us to highlight some unique features of action research. The key words include *better understanding, improvement, reform, problem-solving, step-by-step process* and *modification*. These words also demonstrate the reasons for the popularity of action research as a mode of study for practitioners.

Much of the literature on action research emphasises the practical nature of this type of research. It deals with the practices of people, quite often within their settings. Its main purpose is to improve practice – either one's own practice or the effectiveness of an institution.

I consider action research as a constructive enquiry, during which the researcher constructs his or her knowledge of specific issues through planning, acting, evaluating, refining and learning from the experience. It is a continuous learning process in which the researcher learns and also shares the newly generated knowledge with those who may benefit from it.

Before presenting some examples of action research projects carried out by practitioners, I will summarise the features of action research based on what I have discussed so far.

Action research:

- involves researching your own practice – it is not about people out there;
- is emergent;
- is participatory;
- constructs theory from practice;
- is situation-based;
- can be useful in real problem-solving;
- deals with individuals or groups with a common purpose of improving practice;
- is about improvement;
- involves analysis, reflection and evaluation;
- facilitates changes through enquiry.

As you read the following examples of action research projects, told by the researchers themselves, try to consider how their experiences relate to the different models and definitions presented earlier in this chapter. You may ask yourself whether these examples have elements in common with your own situation and needs.

EXAMPLE 1

Christine, a Year 5 teacher, working in an inner-city school

It was a talk on 'Assessment' I attended at the local teachers' centre that provided the spark for what was to become a year-long action research project. I have responsibility for assessment in my school and, for some time, I was feeling uneasy about the closed nature of the assessment procedures we used. I could not articulate what I wished to change, but after the speaker told us about a study by Black and William on 'Assessment for learning', I felt I could do something about changing things.

'Assessment for learning' emphasises the importance of formative assessment in enhancing children's learning. The speaker talked about some research carried out by the above authors which does suggest that if teachers involved children in their own assessment, it would lead to higher attainment. After the talk, I thought about it and wondered why formative assessment is so powerful and came up with two possible reasons for that. One must be the increased motivation of the students as a result of continuous feedback; the other is the effect it has on more powerful personalised learning through their involvement in the process of learning and assessment.

The first step was to take a good look at what was happening in our school. Children had regular class tests in mathematics and spellings; their work was marked and graded and all the children took the NFER tests at the end of every year. More recently we have also been using the end-of-year national Standard Assessment Tests. As I reflected on what was happening, I recorded 'A world full of tests, to what end?' as my first reaction. Now I had to consider what I wanted to do. Introducing self-assessment as part of everyday learning seemed a good starting point. This was the more challenging part. I felt both excited and nervous. Then it dawned on me that I could undertake a study as part of a practical project for a Masters module which I was studying at the local university. I had not heard of action research before I started. My supervisor suggested that I might try out my ideas as an action research project. So I did.

At the beginning, I was not sure how I was going to conduct a study. Soon I realised I had to ask myself some questions. What was I going to do? What was the purpose? What did I expect to get from the study? Who is going to be involved in the study? What did it entail? One uneasy question that caused me some anxiety was whether there would be opposition from my colleagues who may perceive my ideas as adding to their workload. Finally, I decided to study the outcomes of my ideas with my class and another Year 5 class teacher, with whom I worked closely anyway.

My colleague Alison and I made an initial plan for the study. We listed a sequence of activities such as: read Black and William's paper outlining the benefits of self-assessment and list the benefits. We drew up a schedule to take a close look at what involvement, if any, pupils had in their own assessment. We were horrified by what we found. There was hardly any point in the day where we asked children to comment on what or how they had learnt or how they thought they had done. Assessment in our school seemed to be a mechanical exercise of ticks, grades and marks.

The next step was to decide what to do. We decided to introduce three activities based on our readings. The first was to make children more aware of what the learning intentions of a lesson were. This, we felt, would focus children's learning so they would be more aware of what they were expected to learn and hence would take more resposisibility for their learning. The second was to introduce a weekly diary in which children recorded what they had learnt and how they thought they had learnt and understood something. Another change involved following up what had been said at the session at the teachers' centre; instead of giving a grade for a piece of work, we decided to write a comment. The third activity was to organise a time at the end of the week to discuss the best lessons in the week and let children speak freely about why they thought some lessons had been better than others.

We knew we needed to monitor what happened with each of the three activities. We felt we needed to be realistic and select the kind of data we could manage both in terms of data gathering and analysis. With this in mind, we decided to establish a baseline first.

At the end of two lessons, we asked children what they thought they were supposed to have learnt and write down their responses. We also kept notes on what they had thought they learnt from the two lessons. And finally, we wrote a comment underneath the marks awarded for a piece of work and asked children afterwards what they thought of the comments. While analysing the data we found out that in spite of sharing the learning outcomes with the children they had not taken much notice of these and could not articulate what they were. For the second part, when asked what they had learnt, the responses ranged from two- or three-line vague scribbles to 'don't knows' and in one case 'nothing really', 'I already knew what she [the teacher] was going to teach anyway'. The third set of data was the most revealing. Most children had taken note of their marks and could tell us what their marks were and those of some of their friends too. But they had not read the comments. This was not surprising to us, as I had read about this tendency in the literature.

The intervention activities we had planned were revised in the light of our observations. We decided to photocopy the learning intentions and give copies to the children to stick in their notebooks, so that they would be constantly aware of what they were expected to learn. The second intervention – keeping a learning diary – was found difficult by most children as they were not used to reflecting on their learning. The idea of a general learning diary for all subjects was abandoned and we just concentrated on mathematics lessons only. The third change was to award marks only for some pieces of work and write a set of comments for the others.

The project lasted two terms. We collected evidence of what was happening by discussions between us, through reading our own diary of significant events and generating our interpretations of them. Evidence of children being able to articulate their learning intentions and taking note of the teacher's comments in their workbooks was noted. What we found out from the project outcomes was very useful to us and there was enough evidence for us to see that our activities had yielded some success in achieving more involvement of children with the assessment of their learning.

We were aware that what we had done and found out were useful only to us initially, but during a staff meeting we shared our project with the whole staff and teaching assistants, who were very interested in our findings. At a later stage we gave a presentation to our cluster of schools; the participants were interested especially because we were drawing on practical activities and highlighted what could be achieved within our classes. My colleague is intending to use this project as a basis for her dissertation and for me it was a very hands-on learning experience of 'assessment for learning'.

EXAMPLE 2

Christine – action researcher within an LEA

It all started when, as part of the government's initiative to enhance pro-vision for gifted and talented students, the Department for Education and Skills invited proposals for funding to be awarded to individual schools or groups of practitioners to carry out action research into aspects of nur-turing talents in younger children – specifically children aged 4–7. Brunel University tutors, who had carried out a number of studies into early gift-edness and its development, were invited to guide the action researchers. The purpose of commissioning the project was to generate a knowledge base in gifted education with particular emphasis on children within the first years of schooling. Fourteen groups of practitioners were awarded funding to carry out action research into selected topics. The project pro-vided an opportunity for a group of researchers to work with university academics to explore the best ways of developing talent in younger chil-dren. One of the requirements for providing funding was that the action researchers had to produce case studies of their project and that their findings would be published on the DfES website. Researchers were also invited to present at national conferences organised by the DfES as well as by the university.

We applied for funding to set up a 'pull out' group of exceptionally able pupils whose educational needs, we felt, were not being met within their schools. Schools usually only have one or two of the type of child we had in mind and, within a busy classroom, teachers did not always have the time to devote to them. Some of the children who were referred to the gifted and talented LEA coordinator, Joy, had been showing disruptive behaviour and she felt this may have been due to their frustration caused by having to work on tasks which were cognitively undemanding. Following a successful application for funding, Joy invited me to set up an enrichment cluster. Initially I was nervous when I was told we had to attend some sessions at the university, as my track record of higher educa-tion was not tremendously successful.

Meeting others who were also conducting action research was very useful. The fact that the project was funded by external sources and its

CONTINUED

findings had to be shared with others across the country caused some anxiety, but it also highlighted the importance of having a robust structure and set of outcomes. During the university sessions we discussed action research as a methodology for generating principles based on practice and were reassured by the flexibility it allows.

The first challenge was to identify a focus and decide on what we were hoping to achieve. The outcomes would be useful to colleagues within my own education authority and they should also be of interest to colleagues who may read my case study and listen to my story. Right from the start, I had to remind myself, reinforced by the university staff, that the purpose of the research was not just to help a group of children, but to extract principles and models from the project which may be useful to other practitioners.

A group of 20 children aged 5–6 was selected by their class teachers from a group of schools and sent to the enrichment class run by myself and two assistants from a local school. The group attended a programme of enrichment activities once a week – on Thursday afternoons. The first challenge was to establish a system for the selection of the pupils and this was not easy. My own feeling was that teachers' close observation of children's achievement or potential would be a good starting point. One could always revise this. As it happened, the children who were selected also scored high on a standardised test that we used, suggesting that teachers' judgements were quite accurate.

As it was a new area of exploration for me, I read some research papers on Renzulli's (an expert on enrichment work in schools) enrichment activities which are very popular in the USA. I also received the Brunel tutors' guidance on setting up enrichment activities. In addition, I conducted a web search for other related literature.

A set of activities was planned, taking into account the context of the children's background and the early years policy of the LEA. A local university was involved in providing expertise in some areas of advanced concepts. The project was running smoothly when, during our second meeting, the whole question of how we could evaluate the project came

CONTINUED

up. This part was quite demanding for me and I needed guidance. The first set of questionnaires I designed for parents and teachers needed substantial revision. Triangulation was achieved by seeking perspectives from different persons involved in the project. Photographs were taken and some children were interviewed before, during and at the conclusion of the project. Teachers' views were also gathered.

Our enrichment project was disseminated at a DfES national conference and a display was organised at another conference. The next stage of the project is to share the findings with colleagues at the local teachers' centre. I intend to display some of the children's work and photographs at the centre. I also look forward to writing up the case study and plans are in progress for all the action research partners to contribute a chapter in a book. Dissemination of the processes that we adopted for the action research projects and the outcomes of the project, I am sure, should add to the knowledge base of nurturing talent in the early years of schooling, which is an area where very little research has been done internationally.

EXAMPLE 3

Julian – Year 4 teacher

Like most people, I was excited about the National Numeracy Strategy when it was introduced in 1999. I expected to be 'told' what to teach and what the progression should be. I felt even more impressed that we were given a three-part structure for the daily maths lesson: starting with mental mathematics, followed by the main lesson and concluding with a plenary which was to last about ten minutes. I was broadly happy with this structure at first, but later I became unhappy about my plenary sessions. Those sessions seemed to be unproductive because my children did not actively participate in this part of the lesson. I scrutinised the main purpose of the plenary in the national framework document; it was to assess children's level of understanding of what had been taught, rectify any misconceptions, help them to make connections with previously taught ideas and highlight what progress had been made.

CONTINUED

It was clear that I was not meeting the objectives of the plenary session, as my children were not actively participating within the time designated for the plenary. Either they provided one-word answers to my questions or just kept quiet. At first I was not sure how I would encourage children to participate in the plenary session. I was unhappy about the problem, but did not really know how to solve it. I felt that an opportunity had arisen here; I could choose this topic for investigation in my MA dissertation. Action research, or participatory research, would enable me to work flexibly without a tight and predetermined structure. It would allow me freedom to plan, act, evaluate and refine my ideas before putting them into practice.

As I was embarking on the action research project for the purpose of accreditation for a Master's degree, I knew I had to follow some academic guidelines. I had to undertake a review of the literature on the implementation of the Numeracy Strategy. I also had to demonstrate my understanding of action research and justify why I had chosen it as a method to conduct my research.

My research question was: *How can I make the children in my class take a more active part in the plenary sessions?* Working with my own class to explore strategies made the planning easier. I still had to have a sharp focus on what I wanted to achieve. It took about four weeks of reading and discussion with colleagues and the LEA adviser before I finally made a firm plan. At the planning stage, I needed to set out my aims and objectives. Why was I doing this? What made me want to research into this topic? What evidence should I present in justifying the need to carry out this piece of research?

The first hurdle arose on finding out that literature on my research topic was sparse. As the National Numeracy Strategy was a new initiative, no evaluative literature was available. So I had to justify why I thought there was a problem with the plenary session using my own observations. I used literature on teaching and learning to assess the effectiveness of the sessions in terms of students' motivation and interest; clearly these were missing from my lessons. I constructed a 'do' list:

CONTINUED

- Refer to the objectives of plenary sessions in the documentation provided in the government policy document.

- Collect information about how the objectives are being met in my sessions. Are my concerns borne out by the data?

- Analyse my concerns.

- Plan strategies to encourage active participation.

- Implement strategies.

- Gather data through observations and a personal diary of changes.

- Analyse data for changes and indicators of enhanced understanding of concepts involved in the main lesson.

- Evaluate the effectiveness of the intervention strategies.

I implemented a set of strategies for increasing student participation. One was to reduce the number of closed questions which elicited short and ineffective answers. By asking open-ended questions and using probing techniques, students' responses were more full and their enthusiasm was greater. Another strategy I used was to set questions to be discussed during the main part of the lesson, so that children had time to think about their own learning, which in turn gave them more to talk about. I implemented these strategies in every lesson for three months and collected a good deal of useful data which I analysed and evaluated against my objectives.

As part of the writing up for my dissertation, I knew I had to discuss my findings in relation to the justification for the selection of the topic, its aims and its objectives. My personal learning and the influence the study has had on my practice needed to be highlighted, as well as an acknowledgement of any shortcomings. The way in which my findings could be useful to other practitioners also had to be declared.

I found the methodology of action research highly suitable for my purpose. I was able to work on a topic of personal interest as part of my professional development. The structure allowed me to refine my strategies and directions, as I progressed through the project.

EXAMPLE 4

Nicola – Year 8 teacher

My action research project really started when I first read about a course in Critical Thinking. It was suggested that undertaking a course in Critical Thinking could enhance students' general confidence and performance in other subjects. I was aware that such a claim deserves investigation. My position on the management group of the school gave me enough scope to set up an action research project to explore the influence of teaching Critical Thinking skills on other aspects of children's learning – specifically on their confidence and performance in a range of subjects.

How did I go about it? When I started thinking about trying a Critical Thinking pack with a group of students, I had not really thought about engaging in action research. It was my head teacher who suggested that action research would provide a framework within which I could carry out the study of the effectiveness of Critical Thinking. I read some literature on action research; its underlying principles did seem attractive. Specifically, what drew me to this methodology was the emerging nature of the study. I had a hypothesis based on something I had read and I also knew that Critical Thinking was a hot topic in education. I had an opportunity to test something and make some proposals based on my trials.

I was fortunate in that I did not have to design activities for teaching Critical Thinking, as I had access to a pack designed by two well-known authors. However, from the outset I had to specify that what I would find out from my study would only relate to the particular programme in the Critical Thinking pack. However, some useful principles about the training of students in Critical Thinking could emerge by the time I completed the study.

I am one of those people who like to feel organised before I start anything new. Therefore, I set out the aims of the study. Within action research, I knew what I was setting out to study may need to be revised, but I still felt good when I drew up the following aims for my study:

- to find out what Critical Thinking is all about, the rationale for providing a course for students and the processes involved;

- to search for and read the available literature which claims the benefits of Critical Thinking programmes for secondary school pupils;

- to teach 20 sessions on Critical Thinking to a group of my students, over a period of eight months;

- to monitor any changes in children's level of confidence and performance and also speak to other teachers if they had noticed any changes in the students' performance in other subjects or in any other aspects of their behaviour.

It seemed a lot to do, but I worked out an action plan. The literature search was easy. A visit to a local library provided much information, so did a web search. In fact there was so much information that I had to focus on aspects of Critical Thinking only, rather than other types of thinking skills programmes. In order to narrow the search down even further, I only sought to find literature relating to 12–14-year-old students. The first two aims were broadly achieved within six weeks and the first tangible outcome of the first phase was a handout I produced entitled 'Why Critical Thinking?'

I wanted to set up some visual evidence of any useful findings from my project. With this in mind, I arranged for my teaching sessions to be video recorded. This provided data which could be analysed later. I also monitored students' scores in their other class work – in a range of subjects through other teachers who were not told who were in the Critical Thinking group (I was aware that students themselves may have made this known to others!). I also interviewed some students about their perceptions of the course and collected written evaluations. Comments were sought from the parents of children, though this was not in the original plan. My colleagues were also interviewed. I kept the number of questions to just three and did plenty of probing; the interviews were tape-recorded. Word got out that our school was trialling a new initiative, which generated some interest from local schools as well as from other local education authorities. A positive result of this was the head teacher granting me four weeks' study leave to analyse the massive amount of data I had collected. The analysis led to the writing up of my study which I will be presenting to my colleagues next term. One of the unexpected outcomes was a comment from my colleagues about a change in attitude to learning of the students, though I had not included this feature in my interview schedule. I am sure

CONTINUED

that the school will introduce Critical Thinking as part of the timetable, after everyone has listened to my convincing arguments backed up by evidence. Who knows what will follow after that? It certainly was a worthwhile learning experience for the students and for me.

WHAT ARE THE ADVANTAGES OF ACTION RESEARCH?

A careful study of the case studies presented above highlights some of the advantages of using action research as a method of researching into aspects of practice. Here is list of the advantages that I have compiled. Action research is a powerful and useful model for practitioner research because:

- research can be set within a specific context or situation;

- researchers can be participants – they don't have to be *distant* and *detached* from the situation;

- action research involves continuous evaluation and modifications can be made as the project progresses;

- there are opportunities for theory to emerge from the research rather than always follow a previously formulated theory;

- the study can lead to open-ended outcomes;

- through action research, the researcher can bring a story to life.

THE LIMITATIONS OF ACTION RESEARCH

When you consider action research for the purposes of professional development or improving a situation, it is difficult to list many disadvantages. However, action research is sometimes described as a *soft* option by some, so the researcher needs to define the parameters of the study at the start. Gaining insights and planning action are two of the main purposes of being engaged in action research. There is also the issue of ethical considerations which is of particular significance within action research. Ethical issues are discussed in Chapter 5.

SUMMARY

In this chapter I have tried to give the reader an overview of what is entailed in doing action research. The presentation of models of action research can but give a hint of the flavour of the experience; to digest the nature of action research you need to be an active participant. The academic researchers who have contributed to the development and more widespread acceptance of action research were indicated, their names and publications cited as landmarks in the progress of the methodology. A salient feature of action research is its cyclical structure and this was highlighted by the diagrammatic forms in which four renowned researchers have portrayed their approach to action research. Different readers will, indeed, react to each diagram differently and use them as they fit within their own action plans. The definitions emphasise the role of action research which is possible within the professional and institutional enhancement of the researchers; the attributes and advantages of action research support the positive approach readers are encouraged to adopt. As for the four examples of action research, they are provided as a kind of simulation, enabling readers to become acquainted with the processes and stages prior to experiencing them personally.

Chapter 2

Getting started

KEY POINTS

This chapter focuses on:

- the role of action research in professional development;

- the contexts for action research;

- the concerns relating to the usefulness of action research;

- planning an action research project in practical steps.

INTRODUCTION

In Chapter 1, we explored some features of action research and considered why these features make it a powerful mode of enquiry for practitioners. You should, by now, have a good understanding of the principles which underlie action research and its role in enabling practitioners to reflect on their own practice. The strongest message that I hope has come through by now is that the principal aim of carrying out an action research project is to support a researcher or group of researchers to study an aspect of practice in depth and learn from the experiences. This chapter focuses on the practical aspects of embarking on an action research project. I will try to demonstrate to the reader that with proper guidance and careful planning, all practitioners can undertake action research and enjoy the whole experience.

Before you get started on your action research project, whether it is as part of a funded project or as part of the requirement for an accredited course, it is necessary to consider the following questions:

- What are the features of action research which make it a suitable mode of enquiry for practitioners?

- What are the processes involved in carrying out action research?

- What specific contexts lend themselves to selecting action research as a method of enquiry?

A close look at the above questions should enable you to consider whether you can justify opting for action research as your chosen methodology so as to engage in fruitful discussions about your activities. If you are a student undertaking an action research project as part of an undergraduate or postgraduate course, you will be expected to demonstrate that you have considered the above questions before embarking on your study.

ACTION RESEARCH AND PROFESSIONAL DEVELOPMENT

At this point, let us take a moment to consider the salient features of action research which make it a useful methodology for practitioners by sharing Carr and Kemmis's (1986) list of what action research entails. In their seminal work *Becoming Critical* they view action research as an integral part of critical professional development. The authors list five particular features of action research as a methodology for practitioners. Each of these warrants careful thought and consideration before you take your first step. Some of these ideas were touched on in Chapter 1 but are reinforced here with supporting statements. So, what are these five features? First, the authors assert that action research will entail indicating how it rejects positivist notions of rationality, objectivity and truth in favour of a dialectical view of rationality. Second, it will entail indicating how action research employs the interpretive categories of teachers by using them as a basis for 'language frameworks' which teachers explore and develop in their own theorising. Third, action research provides a means by which distorted self-understandings may be overcome by teachers analysing the way their own practices and understandings are shaped, and the fourth is the linking of reflection to action, offering teachers and others a way of becoming aware of how those aspects of the social order which frustrate rational change may be overcome. Finally, it involves returning to the question of theory and practice, to show that self-critical communities of action researchers enact a form of social organisation in which truth is determined by the way it relates to practice.

Carr and Kemmis's (1986: 162) definition of action research reflects these sentiments:

> A form of enquiry undertaken by participants in social situations in order to improve rationality and justice of their own social or educational practices, as well as their own understanding of these practices and situations in which these practices are carried out.

Let us now consider an all important question: why would a practitioner carry out action research? I can think of several reasons. First, teaching is not about developing a set of technical competencies, although teachers who work with me often say that it is going in that direction! Teaching is concerned with developing young people's minds. This can only be done effectively if the teacher takes time to internalise ideas and this internalisation is more likely to be more effective if it is accompanied by reflection. In recent years the importance of being a reflective practitioner as part of one's professional development has been stressed, not only in the teaching profession, but also for other practitioners in other disciplines – social workers and medical workers, just to name a few. The idea of the teacher's effectiveness being enhanced by being a researcher and being engaged in critical reflection was strongly argued by Stenhouse (1975: 143). He is of the opinion that:

> all well founded curriculum research and development, whether the work of an individual teacher, of a school, of a group working at a teacher's centre or a group working within the co-ordinating framework of a national project, is based on the study of classrooms.

Hopkins (2002: 66) offers a useful dimension to the purpose of carrying out action research. He maintains that 'when we are engaged in classroom research, we can be said to be engaged in educational theorizing, because we are reflecting systematically and critically on practice'. This view helps to dispel the unease felt by many that educational theory which one reads only is too remote from practice. Hopkins quotes two of the fundamental aspects of what Schön (1991) describes as the 'reflective practitioner'. In educational terms, he points out that such professional teachers (a) stand in control of knowledge rather than being subservient to it and (b) by doing this they are engaged in the process of theorising and achieving self-knowledge. Others, such as Hargreaves (1996), have emphasised the concept of teaching as a research-based profession and the importance of evidence-based practice. My own experience with students bears testimony to the freshness and enthusiasm shown by practitioners who have carried out action research and have had opportunities to develop their thinking, and to evaluate and reflect on their practice.

WHAT ARE THE PROCESSES AND OUTCOMES OF ACTION?

Before moving on to the practical task of planning an action research project, let us consider the basic tenets of action research described by O'Leary (2004: 139) who defines action research as:

> A strategy that pursues action and knowledge in an integrated fashion through a cyclical and participatory process. In action research, processes, outcome and application are inextricably linked.

Here is a task for you. You may be considering carrying out an action research project or perhaps you already have a few ideas in mind. Try to consider to what extent your project would involve the following summarised list of processes involved in action research, put forward by O'Leary (2004: 139). For each section, you could pose some questions relating it to your topic and initial plans and perhaps write your thoughts down.

- *Addresses practical problems.* It generally involves the identification of practical problems in a specific context and an attempt to seek and implement solutions within that context. As the project is situated within the workplace, the ownership of change is a priority and the goal is to improve professional practice.

- *Generates knowledge.* The purpose is the production of knowledge to produce change and the enacting of change to produce knowledge.

- *Enacts change.* Changes are incorporated into immediate goals and not left to be implemented after the project.

- *Is participatory.* In action research, researchers collaborate with practitioners and other stakeholders. Contrary to many other research paradigms, action research works *with* rather than *on* or *for* the researched.

- *Is a cyclical process.* Action research is a cyclical process that takes shape as knowledge emerges. Cycles converge towards better situational understanding and improved action implementation, and are based in evaluative practice that alternates between action and critical reflection.

Having considered the processes involved, we now move on to contexts for action research.

CONTEXTS FOR ACTION RESEARCH

A recent study of the published case studies on websites (see section on Useful websites at the end of the book) and those carried out by my own students at the university showed that educational action researchers come from a variety of backgrounds and their topic of study draws on a wide range of subjects. The following examples of action research projects demonstrate the range of topics for action research.

Enhancing classroom practice

These are studies carried out by teachers in their classrooms and focus on an aspect of their practice. Examples are:

- How can I improve my questioning skills?

- Who does most of the talking in my class – the children or me?

- How can I improve children's participation in ICT?

- Will the introduction of a learning diary in mathematics lessons enhance children's conceptual understanding?

- How can I introduce class discussions on children's special interests?

Studying of a particular theme

With new initiatives being announced with increasing frequency by the government, action research offers practitioners an opportunity to try new ideas and evaluate them. Here are some examples:

- What is personalised learning and how can I implement it in my classroom?

- Can we teach problem-solving skills and does the teaching of problem-solving enhance children's performance in other areas of their work?

- What is meant by creativity in the classroom? What is creativity and how can I encourage children to be creative?

- I attended a conference on Multiple Intelligences as a basis of talent development. How do I put into practice what we were told?

Institutional focus

These are topics based in the workplace such as:

- How can we enhance the motivation of our students?

- How can we increase participation at parents' meetings?

- How can we encourage more discussion during staff meetings?

- Take a look at the record-keeping system to make recommendations on how to make it more manageable and useful.

- How can we develop a more caring ethos in the school?

- Are our citizenship lessons having any impact?

- Devise anti-bullying strategies and monitor their effectiveness.

Implementation of a new initiative

Action research is carried out by a group of practitioners who select a new initiative, study its practical implications, consider ways of implementing the ideas, and evaluate and make decisions based on the collective experiences of participants, before reporting it to other colleagues within the education authority. Examples are:

- Setting up a learning mentor scheme and producing a set of guidlines for schools on how to implement them effectively.

- How can we make school-based in-service sessions more effective?

- Adopting the new *assessment for learning* framework.

ACTION RESEARCH AS PURPOSEFUL RESEARCH

I quoted the views of a practising teacher, Laura, in the Introduction to this book, who used to feel that research was for the lucky few who pursued academic careers. Carrying out an action research project brought it home to her that it was possible for practising teachers to experience the research process and benefit from that experience. In recent years, concern has been expressed by many (Hargreaves, 1996; Rose, 2002) that education research was not always reaching the practitioners, as quite often work done by academics was published in journals generally not read by them. In this context it is worth pointing out that action research opens up opportunities for practitioners to actually be involved in research, which has immediate relevance and application. A study of the stated aims of the teacher-researcher scheme (1997–2001) offered by the Teacher Training Agency (1998) reflects one of the many efforts being made to make teaching a research-based profession. The aims of the teacher-researcher scheme presented below are worthy of consideration:

- To encourage teachers to engage with research and evidence about pupils' achievements, for example to use other people's research to inform their practice and/or to participate actively in research.

- To increase the capacity for high-quality, teacher-focused classroom research by supporting teacher involvement in the development of research proposals for external funding.

- To support teachers in designing, applying and for carrying out more medium and large-scale classroom-based research about pedagogy where teachers have an active role.

- To enable experiments in disseminating research findings and making use of them in classrooms.

- To provide examples of good practice in making use of research.

IS ACTION RESEARCH REAL RESEARCH?

Before starting out, the action researcher should also be aware of some of the criticisms raised against action research and how these can be dealt with in the context of both setting up a project and disseminating the outcomes. What are the concerns raised by critics? Let us consider each of the following headings and respond to these concerns.

Concern 1: Action research lacks rigour and validity

My response to this concern is that it is possible to be rigorous in both gathering and analysing data within action research. The work is located within one's context and acknowledged as such. Therefore drawing on national samples is not a requirement. By using a variety of research methods used in traditional research, the action researcher can carry out the work keeping to strict standards. Sharing data with critical friends and triangulation would ensure that the quality of what is gathered is robust and without bias.

Concern 2: Action research findings are not generalisable

Many of my students have been anxious about the issue of generalisability within action research. My argument is that the action researcher does not set out to seek generalisable data, but to generate knowledge based on action within one's own situation. Any findings from the research are generalisable only within that situation and within the context of the work, which is declared in advance. Dissemination of findings could be applicable to those who are interested and to other practitioners in similar circumstances, either locally or at a distance. It may be useful also for those who wish to apply the findings or replicate the study. I always compare the dissemination of a case study within an action research project to showing a documentary for raising issues; this can be very powerful.

Concern 3: It is a deficit model

Quite often, reference is made to the problem-solving nature of action research which may portray the process as a deficit model. This is not so. First, developing strategies for solving a problem within a situation is not negative action, it really is about making progress and the development of ideas.

MAKING A START

Whether you are a practitioner at the stage of making an application for external funding for a project, or an undergraduate or postgraduate student planning a topic for a special study which leads to a dissertation, thorough planning can reduce much of the anxiety one may feel at the start. Although most of the models of action research presented in Chapter 1 describe action research as cyclical in nature, my students often tell me that some awareness of what may happen during the project, represented in distinct stages, helps them to have an overview of the whole process to plan more efficiently. But you need to bear in mind that any model of suggested progression does not always necessarily guarantee that your project will follow that order. It is just helpful to think about the stages so as to gain some insight into what to expect.

So, what may be the stages? The following list may be helpful:

- Identifying a topic and setting the context
- Reviewing and analysing the literature
- Focusing on the topic, question or hypothesis
- Planning activities
- Gathering data
- Analysing data
- Acting/implementing
- Reflecting on outcomes
- Reporting.

Rather than dealing with the above stages separately, I will try to discuss these stages under three broad headings which incorporate them all:

i. Identifying a topic

ii. Moving on

iii. Practical considerations

IDENTIFYING A TOPIC

The first task for an action researcher is to select a topic for investigation or enquiry. It is very likely that you have not yet come to a decision on what to study. It is perfectly natural for a beginner to have a number of topics in mind. It is often useful to write them down. Your ideas may have come to you from a number of contexts. It may be that you have read an article or a book about a new idea. Often, a new directive from the government sparks off an interest to look at its implications in practice. It is possible that your interest in exploring a topic arose as a result of being given responsibility for a particular subject area or because you have been placed within a new managerial role. Or, as a teacher-trainee, you have several ideas buzzing in your head that you want to explore. In some cases you may be asked by an education authority or your institution to undertake research in order to evaluate the effectiveness of a particular initiative or a new theme. In all these cases, one thing that is common is relevance to your professional development.

Taking the first step

If you are in the process of selecting a topic for research, it is a good idea to write a list of topics which are of interest to you before selecting the one that you feel strongly about; that is something which is very personal to you. During the introductory session on action research, I usually ask my students to write down their first thoughts on topics and why they feel the topics are important to them. Students first talk about their initial choices, in groups, and they find this a useful process in helping them to focus on a particular topic or aspect of a topic. Here is an example of what Helen, one of my undergraduate students, wrote:

I have *three* topics in mind that I would like to choose from. First is the way my class is grouped into ability groups at present. I wondered if children's attitudes may be affected by being put in a particular group for all the lessons, especially if they are in a lower ability group. Although they are never referred to as lower ability, they often tell me that they are the 'dunce' group and mess about too much. I can see why it is necessary to group them for some lessons, but I want to find out whether their attitude to work and the quality of their work will be different if they work with children who are more able, at least for other lessons. Perhaps I could try a different grouping strategy for topic work ...

My second topic is to try some problem-solving activities with children. I feel that the children learn much of what I teach them by rote, and do very little thinking ...

The third topic I am interested in is creative writing. A number of children seem to be really turned off during this lesson. I would like to introduce some new stimulus and record any changes in their attitude and in what they produce ...

Rachel, a secondary teacher who was planning to apply for external funding from the government for an action research project, wrote:

As I am the co-ordinator for Information Technology, I want to work on something to do with IT, but I am not sure what, yet. Here are some thoughts.

- The first question: Do students make good use of the ICT facilities in the school?

- Second one: How I can improve students' use of the Internet for their project work? At the moment they seem to just print out so much, but do not actually know how to make use of all the information.

- The third one is about assessing the effectiveness of ICT software packages that we buy. There are so many companies producing software and different departments buy them, but we have never really evaluated their usefulness or how we can make effective use of these packages.

After talking through her ideas with other members of the group who raised questions, Helen decided to undertake a study of the creative writing topic. The discussion of Rachel's ideas took a long time. It was interesting to see Rachel being challenged on the very general nature of her first idea as not being feasible within a relatively short period of time. Rachel's third idea involving several departments, again, was felt to be difficult to carry out within the time constraints of a funded project lasting just a few months.

Discussion of your ideas with others can often help focus your thoughts to consider the feasibility of carrying out a study on a particular topic, its sensitivity and practical implications.

Finally, it may also be the case that you decide to select your action research topic for other reasons. For example, you may be facing dilemmas about something – whether to use a particular published scheme or resource or to improve the recording of assessment within your classroom.

Critical appraisal of topics for action research

As part of a research training session, my colleague and I asked our students to comment on the possibility of undertaking action research on the following topics. Some of these were chosen deliberately to generate discussion – in some cases very heated ones! Study each of these (you may want to do this with one or two colleagues) and try to write down some comments before reading the examples of comments we gathered from our students during the session. This exercise was not designed to provide definitive answers, but to promote discussion.

i.   Factors contributing to effective learning.

ii. Implementing an accelerated learning model in my classroom.

iii. Improving my questioning strategies.

iv. Monitoring the bullying of women teachers in my institution by male teachers.

v.   A comparison of mathematics performance test results across three local education authorities in our neighbourhood.

vi. Extending able children through after-school activities.

Commentary

i. The first topic was considered too general for an action research project in its present from. It was suggested that the researcher could identify factors that contribute to effective learning from existing research or other literature and plan some intervention activities based on these factors. The activities could be presented to a selected group of pupils and their progress monitored. The importance of keeping the project small and focused was stressed. So was the challenge of designing a method for judging the effectiveness of strategies for effective learning.

ii. Accelerated learning strategies have been the subject of many conferences in recent years and it was felt that action research offers an ideal way for implementing the principles and continuously monitoring what was happening. Action research provides opportunities for the researcher to refine strategies and make adjustments as the project progresses. It was felt that this topic would provide opportunities for dissemination to colleagues, using evidence collected during the project.

iii. The third topic – improving one's questioning strategies – received positive comments in terms of its potential as a subject for action research. The personal nature of the investigation, it was felt, would make it an ideal topic for professional development and improvement of practice. The need for explaining what was meant by 'improving' was stressed and strategies for establishing a baseline of current practice was also felt necessary.

iv. This topic resulted in the noisiest discussion. Questions were raised which included: *Who says there is bullying by male teachers? How could this be studied anyway? Even if it is true, is it too sensitive a topic to make the findings public? Who is going to co-operate with this kind of topic?*

v. This topic was described as being beyond the scope of an action research project for several reasons: it would take too long and it would involve analysis of much quantitative data. One of the main purposes of carrying out action research – improvement of practice – was unlikely to take a prominent role within this topic.

vi. The last topic was found suitable for action research. It could focus on a small, manageable group. What was meant by enrichment activities had to be defined and explantions would need to be provided as to how able children may be selected. This project, they felt, could fit into an action research cycle of selecting a topic, reviewing existing literature, planning activities, evaluating and reflecting. It provided opportunities for refining the activities responding to the ongoing gathering of evidence.

Having selected a topic for investigation, it may be necessary to consider different aspects of the topic to help you to fine-tune it before you start your study. But do remember, many action researchers also recognise the need to fine-tune their topic after reading some related literature or after thinking about the practical implications of carrying out the study.

Here is an example of refining a topic of study. Melanie selected her action research topic: *Introducing portfolios of learning for year 7 students.* During her discussion with colleagues it was pointed out to her that the topic was too wide for action research. It was suggested that Melanie needed to narrow her focus and perhaps concentrate on one aspect of her topic. She then generated some sub-questions within the general topic of the use of portfolios, such as:

- What are portfolios?

- Do portfolios enhance my pupils' motivation for learning?

- Can I involve parents in developing their children's portfolios?

After some consideration she decided that the third question was more likely to suit the format of action research.

Examples of topics

In this section I have included some examples of action research projects. Some of these are from my own students and others are examples of projects funded by the DfES and other sources I have read about. The purpose of including them is twofold. First, it shows the range of topics practitioners have selected for their research and, second, it shows the different types of titles people have used. Some are in the form of a question, or a hypothesis and others relate to specific aspects of practice.

- How can I improve communications between staff in my role as a senior manager?

- An enquiry into the feasibility of adopting the Italian 'Reggio Emelia' programme in an early years classroom in England.

- Design and evaluation of an intervention programme to enhance children's understanding of subtraction.

- Using group work to encourage creativity.

- The use of music as a stimulus for creative writing. What are the outcomes?

- Children in my class – aged 5 years old – making big books and leading class discussions.

- Introducing problem-solving in mathematics lessons and monitoring any changes in children's attitudes and achievement in mathematics.

- The attitudes of boys and girls to creative writing.

- Does homework enhance student achievement?

- Developing and evaluating activities which promote talk among children with English as an Additional Language.

- Developing a system for formative feedback in English lessons.

- Can encouraging imagery support mental mathematics?

- What do students feel about their algebra lessons?

MOVING ON

After selecting a topic, the next set of useful questions to ask are:

- What is currently happening in the area which I intend to investigate?

- What am I expecting from the project?

- What can I actually do about it?

- How would I go about it?

● What information will I need?

● Have I got the resources I require?

A very useful question to consider here is whether it is possible to make any changes that you may wish to after the project has been completed. For example, one of my Master's students was feeling uneasy about the introduction of the National Literacy Strategy and wished to undertake a study, hoping to make recommendations as to whether they should continue to follow the strategy in his school. Soon he realised that very little could be done, if he wished, to persuade his school to abandon a National Literacy Strategy and that his time and efforts would be better employed to working on ways to make the strategy more effective in terms of children's motivation and learning.

Similarly, if it is LEA policy to set targets for all its schools, any effort spent on an action research project to resist it may be a waste of energy and valuable time. I am not discouraging readers from undertaking research in controversial areas, as long as the purpose is greater under-standing of issues relating to the topic or the identification of factors which could lead to fruitful discussions with others who may be inter-ested. In relation to the National Literacy Strategy, for example, any contribution in terms of an analysis of its purpose and the practical aspects of its delivery could be of immense value to both policy-makers and practitioners.

PRACTICAL CONSIDERATIONS

In this section we will look at some other practical issues that an action researcher needs to consider.

Experience and interest

A topic for action research is often located within a researcher's experi-ence and context. It needs to be grounded in the realities of the workplace. Ask yourself if you are sufficiently interested in the topic of investigation to devote a considerable amount of time and effort to it. In my experience, I find personal interest and passion for a topic to be important factors which motivate an action researcher. I have witnessed many animated action researchers who have carried out enquiries on subjects which were meaningful and relevant to their situations.

The research question

If your action research involves investigating a question, you need to consider the type of question which is appropriate to ask. A consideration of what your expected outcomes are may help you in phrasing your question. You will need to consider whether your question is specific or open-ended in nature. You may wish to explore a specific question and expect multiple outcomes from your project. It may be that you have a hypothesis to explore. A hypothesis can be be based on a tentative, speculative conjecture about an issue which you wish to investigate, or it may be based on an intuitive insight about an idea which then needs to be explored. I always feel that a hypothesis arising from the curiosity of the researcher is worthy of investigation, but I emphasise the importance of data-gathering within the context of action research. You need to be open-minded in your collection and analysis of data, but also bear in mind what kind of data needs to be collected in order to draw any conclusions.

Scope and resources

Remember that an action research project needs to be focused and is often a small-scale investigation. You need to select topics which are manageable and which support your professional development. I often tell my students that they are not likely to change the world through an action research project, but may bring about an improvement in their own practice or implement some changes within their institution. Ask yourself what you can possibly achieve in the timescale available to you. Be realistic. You also need to consider external factors that may affect the project. For example, do you have enough resources to carry out your project? Consider this question in terms of availability of time, people and physical materials. Do you, for example, have support for word processing or transcribing tapes? You also need to consider whether you are likely to change your job during the scheduled time of the project or if your institution intends to embark on another initiative which will require your time.

Planning

The importance of planning cannot be overemphasised. Make your aims clear and list your objectives unambiguously. Plan activities which relate to the achievement of your objectives. Spend time considering the kind of data you will need to collect and the processes involved in the data collection. It is useful to initiate a literature search as soon as you have a selected a topic and to start making notes and summaries. In the light of what you read, it may be necessary for you to refine or even change your topic.

Working collaboratively

An important feature of action research is that it offers opportunities for collaborative work. The need for collaboration and co-operation is of paramount importance for the success of your project. You may be part of a group of action researchers. Whether you are leading the project or contributing to the project, teamwork is essential. If you are in a leadership role, it is important to show that you value everyone's contributions. If you are a co-researcher it is necessary to listen and share perspectives as often as you can possibly manage it. I encourage my students to set up a list of critical friends who are willing to discuss their work, look at the documentation, provide their perspectives and offer advice where they can. The role of critical friends is helpful in maintaining rigour and the quality of your findings. But remember that it is not always easy to accept critical comments on what you have spent hours preparing or doing. The need for establishing trust and respect for your critical friends is, therefore, paramount.

Consider dissemination

Finally, do consider the question: what will I do with my findings when the project is complete? It is important from the start to think about how you would disseminate the project findings. It may be that you will need to send a report to the funding body. There may be a specific format you will need to follow. Are you intending to make a conference presentation or lead a professional development course? Would you consider writing for a professional journal? You may be doing this project as part of your study at a university leading to a dissertation. In all these cases, it will be useful to cast your eyes forward and think about the final outcomes. I remember one of my action researchers sharing her folder of children's work and photographs with me which she had been collecting from the start of the project to use on a course she was 'expected' to deliver at the local teachers' centre.

SUMMARY

In the first half of this chapter I made a case for action research by highlighting its value for educational enhancement. I tried to address some of the criticisms levelled against action research and explained its purpose in terms of improving practice. The five features of action research proposed by Carr and Kemmis may appear complex, but they do provide the essence of what is involved in the search for truth, through action research, and will steer you towards practical benefits for practitioners and the recipients of the process of education. Also O'Leary's indicators of structure and processes may be linked to the cyclical model depicted in Chapter 1.

The second half of the chapter guides the reader towards the first steps of enquiry into educational reality. The advice provided on the selection of a research topic and its refinement and revision resulting from discussions with colleagues should make a significant contribution to a harmonious, collaborative working environment, whether the action research is to be directed towards the improvement of performance of an individual, or a practical aspect of implementing new educational initiatives within a classroom, institution or education authority.

Chapter 3

Reviewing literature

INTRODUCTION

Assume you have selected an area of study for your action research. Your aim is to generate new knowledge for yourself and to share your findings with others. Reviewing what literature is out there on your topic of research is an important part of conducting all forms of research. You need to consider this aspect now that you are about to embark on your enquiry. As O'Leary (2004: 66) points out, the 'production of new knowledge is fundamentally dependant on past knowledge' and that 'it is virtually impossible for researchers to add to a body of literature if they are not conversant with it'. O'Leary's assertion provides an appropriate background to this chapter:

> ...working with literature is an essential part of the research process. It inspires, informs, educates and enlightens. It generates

ideas, helps form significant questions, and is instrumental in the process of research design. It is also central to the process of writing-up; a clear rationale supported by literature is essential, while a well constructed literature review is an important criterion in establishing researcher credibility.

Why do we need to find out what others have done in your area of research? Reading about what others have found out about your topic of research can help you in several ways. It can enhance your understanding of the issues associated with the topic. It can also help you to sharpen the focus of your study. My students have often refined or fine-tuned their research question or hypothesis after reading around the topic.

Reading around the topic will help you to gain insights into the topic as well as guide you in the pursuit of fruitful activities. The time spent on searching for literature could in fact optimise the benefits of your research and support you with the structure and quality of your enquiry. It may help you to decide whether a line of enquiry is appropriate and feasible. Here I am not discouraging you from pursuing a topic of study which has been researched before, on the assumption that 'there is no need to reinvent the wheel'. If you find a similar study to the one you are about to undertake, you could replicate it within your own context using an appropriate set of methods. This may help you assess whether a set of findings generated from a different study is applicable to your context. Whatever the outcome of your research, we need to remind ourselves that the action researcher generates knowledge as a means to continuing professional development.

Here are some more reasons why your literature search and review could help you in your action research. Getting to know the literature relating to your study should:

- help you to identify what has been done before and any gaps;

- provide a background to your enquiry and help you to articulate a rationale for the study;

- support you in reviewing and refining your research topic, question or hypothesis;

- enable you to locate your project within current debates and viewpoints;

- provide a backcloth for your study;

- help you to analyse your findings and discuss them with rigour and scholarship.

While it is good to read as much as you can about your topic of study, you also need to be realistic in terms of what you can manage. It is also helpful to consider what is expected of you. Again, your personal circumstances will have some bearing on the decision as to the extent of your literature search.

If you are carrying out action research as part of an accredited study such as a Master's or a taught doctorate programme, you will be expected to present a comprehensive review of literature and demonstrate your understanding of the issues around the topic. The research literature should help you to build up a framework for the fieldwork you are about to undertake, as well as provide a basis for further discussion of the issues after the data has been collected and analysed. You would be asking how your data relate to the findings and theories put forward by others.

If you are undertaking a small-scale action research project as part of a local initiative or as an externally funded project, you will still need to read about your topic as it will help you to contextualise your study within existing literature. In this case you may want to focus on a smaller, more relevant range of literature. So, to summarise, an action researcher needs to undertake a literature search and analysis in order to understand, locate, plan and evaluate a study more effectively.

This chapter will explore ways in which an action researcher may go about searching for literature - both theory and research – by providing some practical suggestions.

WHAT KINDS OF LITERATURE?

There are various forms of literature you will need to consider. The following sections discuss a selection.

Policy-related literature

This includes official documents which outline education policy which the practitioner needs to be familiar with. For example, a recent major initiative within secondary schools such as *Excellence in Cities* (DfEE, 1999) has several strands to it and you may be researching into one of these strands. If your research topic is to do with mentoring, reading the relevant official documents will help you to understand the rationale and the context of the initiative. The rationale provided in these documents – justified in terms of theory and research – may spark off new ideas in your mind. You may also find papers which address the issues around the new initiatives in professional journals. Recent newspaper articles can often provide you with insights into new initiatives. These insights will be useful to you in setting up the context or background for your work.

Theoretical literature

Locating your research within a theoretical background is important. Even if you are only engaged in a small-scale project, it is extremely useful to locate any theoretical views which underlie what you are about to research. If your research forms part of a degree or accredited module, your tutors should provide you with guidance during lectures and give you appropriate reading lists. For example, if your study focuses on the role of adult mentors in enhancing children's learning, you would certainly be advised to read Vygotski's (1978) work on Zone of Proximal Development which explains how a child's potential is more effectively realised with adult support.

Existing research

A third type of literature you could be seeking comprises existing research findings on your chosen topic. Who else may have studied a similar theme? There is a vast amount of research literature available in research journals which are often accessible electronically. These range from large-scale studies to findings of action research projects carried out by other researchers such as yourself. You will find it useful to read about the research findings of others and also to take note of the methodology they have used for their studies. You may wish to focus on the most recent of these sources. Useful sources of reference, for the new researcher, are the websites of the National College of Leadership, the Department for Education and Skills, the Qualifications and Curriculum Authority and others (see the Useful websites section at the end of the book) where you should find useful information on new initiatives and details of related research.

Research methods

When you are reading research literature, take note of the research methods used by other researchers, especially if the study was carried out as action research. This will support you with methods for data-gathering and analysis. Make a critical appraisal of the methodology used by others. Ask yourself whether the data-gathering methods were appropriate. Was the data analysed effectively? Are the findings presented clearly?

WHERE DO YOU SEARCH FOR LITERATURE?

Before considering ways in which you can search for literature relating to your study, let me share with you what my students often tell me. One student told me that her search for literature generated such a large amount of information that she was quite overwhelmed by it. This is partly the result of the Internet age we live in and the facilities for fast information retrieval. What you need to do is to skim read to find out what is being offered and select a few sources which are directly relevant to the topic of your research.

Where do you search for literature? If you are a student at a university undertaking a course for a qualification, or if your small-scale research is supervised by a university tutor, your library would be the most useful and accessible place for you to start. Most libraries have good systems for accessing literature in the form of books and journals; you can also access research papers electronically using key word searches. For example, if your research topic is 'Adult mentoring for enhancement of learning', using key words such as *mentor* and *adult support* will generate abstracts of papers from national and international journals. You can then decide which papers are directly relevant and useful to your study.

And don't forget that journals and newsletters of professional organisations are other sources for your search. If you are not working with a university, your local library still can help you with your literature search through inter-library loans. In recent times I have found a web search to be very productive in terms of tracking down a range of references.

University-based research and development centres and their websites are also helpful sources of recent information. They publicise conferences and seminars which you may wish to attend so that you can listen to experts in the field that you are researching. Education journals and newspapers also can provide information on conferences and courses which you may wish to attend.

TAKE NOTE ...

If you are an action researcher reading about action research carried out by other practitioners, take note of the following:

- What was the context of their research?

- Who was involved? Was it a collaborative project?

- Was the choice of using action research as a method justified? Are any models discussed?

- What 'actions' did actually take place?

- How was data gathered?

- How was data analysed?

- Were ethical considerations addressed? How?

- What were the conclusions? Were they justified using appropriate evidence?

- Was the report accessible? Useful?

- Is it possible to replicate the study?

ORGANISING YOUR LITERATURE

Suppose you have gathered a good range of literature on your topic. Your challenge then is to organise your collection and make it manageable and useful. Bear in mind that you will also need to access your readings at the time of writing up. Try to be meticulous about keeping a record of what you are reading in terms of references to the texts or articles. Organise summaries of what you have read. I remember the time, during my own doctoral studies, how I wished that I had been more organised with my collection of literature. I used to read and think about the content of what I had read and store a copy of it in a box file, thinking that I would be able to go back and find the references at the time of writing up. This strategy proved inefficient and resulted in me wasting a lot of time. As I read more, the more difficult and more chaotic it became. Sometimes it was very frustrating and time-consuming trying to track down the references I required!

It may sound like stating the obvious, but organising your literature search efficiently from the start is vital. Here is a practical suggestion using the example of the research topic I used earlier – investigating effective ways in which school mentors can be involved in enhancing children's learning. Suppose you managed to get two journal articles from the library and a printout of the outline of a similar project from a website. Assume you also obtained a printout of a summary of the *Excellence in Cities* initiative from the DfES website which refers to the role of mentors. After you have read its contents you decided to send for the whole document *Excellence in Cities* (DfEE, 1999). A further search on the web generated more references on this particular topic. For example, a recent report from the school inspectorate, evaluating the Excellence in Cities initiative, could be sent for. Now you have several references to record. One of the simple ways of organising all these sources of information is for you to record them on index cards. You need to record the title of the book, chapter or paper, author, date, nature of the content and a short commentary, including any direct quotes you may wish to include at a later date. The simple examples in Figures 3.1, 3.2 and 3.3 illustrate what I mean.

Figure 3.1 Example of recording a reference: a government document.

Author/source: Department for Education and Employment (DfEE)

Title: *Excellence in Cities*

Date: 1999

Description/key issues: Launched by the Labour govt to improve achievement of students in inner-city areas. *Use of 'mentors'* is a key area within this initiative.

Quote: Page ... lines ... is useful as a direct quote.

Follow up: Has there been any evaluation of this initiative?

Figure 3.2 Example of recording a reference book.

Author: Koshy, V.

Title: *Effective Teaching of Numeracy*

Date: 1999

Publisher: Hodder and Stoughton

Description/key issues: This book outlines and critiques the National Numeracy Strategy. Pages 53–78 address issues on mental mathematics. The author deals with some strategies teachers can use for teaching mental mathematics.

Quote: Page 53 – a definition of mental mathematics.

Follow up: The author refers to Askew's Nuffield research project.

Figure 3.3   Example of recording a chapter in a book.

Author: Reynolds and Muijs (eds)

Title: *Effective Teaching*

Chapter: 2. Interactive teaching

Publisher: Paul Chapman

Description/key issues: ...

Useful quotes: Page (...)

Follow up: ...

I find the use of index cards a very practical and simple way of keeping track of what I have read but, if you have a good knowledge of technology, you may be able to set up systems using your computer which will do the same as index cards. In that case, information retrieval and storage will be much quicker. Having said all this, the most effective recording system will be one which is personal and manageable for you. You may want to take note of the above guidelines and then design your own systems.

REVIEWING THE LITERATURE

Assume now that you have collected and read some literature which relates to your study. At this stage, it may be useful to have a quick look at Chapter 7, where I discuss how you may present the literature review in your final report. So far, for each book or paper that you have read you have written down some key issues. If you find two or more authors agree or disagree on some ideas, do make a note of this, using high-lighters or coloured pens. This will help you when it is time for writing up your research. As I have emphasised in Chapter 7, there is nothing worse than providing a list of what different authors have said without a connecting thread going through them. Remind yourself that one important purpose of searching for different sources of literature and reviewing them is to help you to construct a framework for understanding the issues relating to your topic of investigation. This is most effectively done if you can tell a coherent story which emerges from your readings.

During one of our detailed discussions at the university on how to write a literature review, my students came up with a format which you may find useful. They proposed a three-stage plan as follows:

i.   Identify the significant themes that have emerged from your readings. These would have been highlighted through written summaries and colour-coded sections while you were gathering and reading the literature.

ii. Introduce the ideas by themes rather than by listing different authors' viewpoints. If you write in sequence what others have said it can become very tedious and disjointed for the reader.

iii. Introduce each theme and explain what that particular theme is. Then present the evidence from your readings, both agreements and disagreements between experts. For example, if you are discussing the theme of using portfolios as a means to raise student achievement, explain what the particular theme means in this context and put forward the views of authors and experts on that theme followed by a critical commentary of what you think.

In this context Blaxter *et al.*'s (1996: 115) guidance to researchers on writing critical reviews of literature is worthy of consideration. The suggestion is that you use your references to:

- justify and support your arguments;

- allow you to make comparisons with other research;

- explain matters better than you could have done;

- explain your familiarity with your field of research.

O'Leary's representation, in Figure 3.4, provides an effective diagrammatic model of how the research process is supported by a literature search and its use. I will exemplify this model through the work of one of my students, Claire.

Figure 3.4 Working with literature.

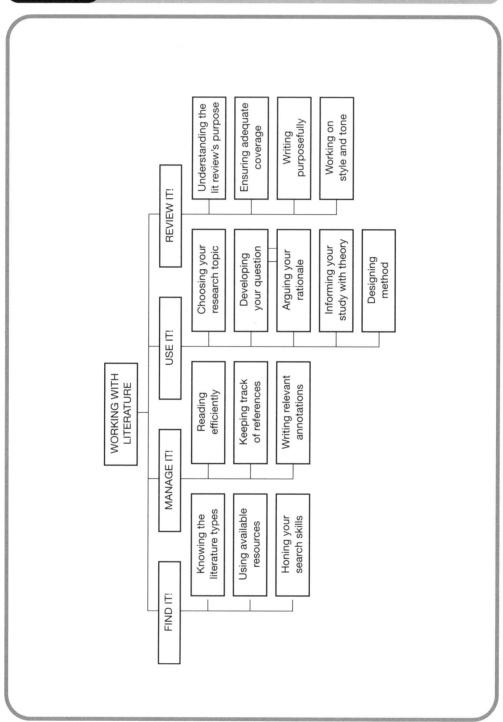

For Claire, the spark of interest in her topic was provided when she read the result of a survey which claimed that the examination results of students who had attended problem-solving sessions improved by 24 points in mathematics and 22 points in science. Claire became interested in the topic of problem-solving, but at this stage it just stayed as an interest for quite some time. Then, after a staff meeting which discussed the different ways boys and girls approached open-ended work, she decided to search for literature to find out more about problem-solving. She read a range of books, including textbooks. She searched websites and accidentally came across the World Class Tests in Problem-solving, offered by the Qualifications and Curriculum Authority. It was a coincidence that at that time she was considering studying for a module on action research at the local higher education institution, and this gave her a context for carrying out a further investigation into the topic of problem-solving.

Developing a research question

Claire knew that her topic of study could be related to problem-solving, but at this stage she needed more knowledge about the topic. More searches and reading a range of literature helped her to identify an area for action research. She decided to study how boys and girls approached problem-solving.

Articulating a context

The original rationale for the research question was her personal interest in the topic. Then further reading directed her to research findings which suggested that boys scored higher marks in problem-solving than girls. She decided to design an intervention programme of problem-solving and monitor the outcomes to find out whether there are differences in the performance of boys and girls when they solve problems. Her own studies also provided considerable impetus to her motivation to carry out a structured small-scale investigation.

Informing your study with theory

It was time for more reading. Claire tracked down readings – both theoretical texts and existing research literature – on three subjects which related to her research topic: *gender, achievement* and *problem-solving*. Informed by all three sets of readings she was able to proceed to her action research project with more confidence.

Designing the method

Claire decided to carry out an action research project which allowed her the flexibility to refine her activities as a result of evaluation and reflection at each stage of her work. With a complex topic involving several strands to the exploration, the issue of flexibility was reassuring to her. Reading and analysing the literature also informed her about possible ways of collecting data. For example, she knew that she needed to establish a baseline so that comparisons of pre- and post-intervention results could be made.

Writing a literature review

Claire made systematic notes on the key issues discussed in the books and papers she read. She developed the themes she had identified within the literature and made critical comments on different issues. This process not only helped her to feel more well-informed about the topic of her study, but she also felt more prepared for writing up her final report at the end of the project.

SUMMARY

After the first step of making a start with action research described in Chapter 2, this chapter has led you through the process of searching for relevant literature. Guidance has been given on how to structure the search and organise the literature. Three kinds of literature were specified relating to policy, theory and related research publications. It was also proposed that the fledgling researcher take note of research methods used by other researchers and critically appraise their findings. In this chapter I have attempted to suggest ways in which the action researcher can ease the path through the literature maze.

Chapter 4

Planning action

KEY POINTS

This chapter takes you through the planning stage by focusing on:

- listing the stages of an action research project;

- making use of tutorials;

- using exemplar case studies for guidance.

INTRODUCTION

The previous two chapters of this book focused on various kinds of preparation an action researcher makes before implementing action. You are now at the stage of having selected a topic and reflected on different aspects of that topic. You have undertaken a literature search and have done some reading which has enriched your understanding of different issues relating to the topic. As a result of your reading and further thinking, you may have changed or fine-tuned your topic of investigation. Now it is time for action. In this chapter, I will address many of the practical issues of carrying out action research, drawing on some personal experiences of supervising practitioner-researchers in different settings.

Carrying out action research is a rewarding experience. But a good action research project does not happen by accident; it needs careful planning, flexibility of approach and continuous reflection on the part of the researcher. Although action research does not have to go through a predetermined set of steps, it is useful for the researcher to be aware of the progression which I presented in Chapter 2. The sequence of activities I suggested there could be looked on as a checklist for you to consider before planning the practical aspects of the project.

Here is a checklist for the action researcher who is about to plan action:

- Have you identified a topic for study?

- Have you set a context for the study? It may be within the professional development of you as a person, or in the context of change within your institution.

- Have you read some relevant literature?

- Have you refined and focused on a research question?

- Have you assessed the resource implications?

Before you start the project, it is useful to write down:

- the title;

- the background of the study, both in terms of professional context and personal motivation;

- the aims;

- the specific outcomes you are hoping for.

Having discussed the stages of action research, I need to remind the reader of the cyclical nature of action research. Most of the models of action research presented in Chapter 1 suggest action taking place in some order, but they also allow us the possibility of refining our ideas and action in the light of our experiences. Changes may need to be made in response to your evaluation and your reflections on how the project is progressing. For example, you may need to make adjustments, taking into account the children's responses and comments and observations from your colleagues. This is quite common and useful. In fact, it is this feature of action research which makes it suitable for practitioner research.

MAKING PREPARATIONS

Here is a practical task for you to try. Read the following case study of a project written by an action researcher that I supervised for the funding body which sponsored the project. The format is not the focus of your task, as I am sure it could have been presented in a different way. Read the case study and construct a detailed list of action which could have been planned in advance. Your list can also include preparations. You may find it useful to annotate the text in pencil while reading it. Then compare it with the actual 'do list' made by the researcher which I have presented later.

Title of project:
Can we improve performance by introducing a problem-solving approach to mathematics teaching?

BACKGROUND

Our school is an 11–18 school in an inner-city area which draws its pupils from mainly council-owned housing. In recent years the mathematics achievement of pupils has been low. The new head of mathematics suggested that Year 7 teachers organise an intervention programme of teaching specific problem-solving skills as a way of improving achievement. The school was successful in obtaining a small grant from a local business to enable a group of teachers to undertake an action research project. A mathematics lecturer from a local teacher training institution was recruited to provide leadership.

INITIAL OBSERVATIONS

During the preparatory stage, the group of action researchers observed their students' responses and made notes. Students' strategies for tackling mathematics work were noted. Their written work was analysed. Based on the initial data it was noticeable that most were quite comfortable in producing correct answers to routine work, such as the four operations on numbers, including fractions and decimals. Students' strategies were based on the rote-learning of rules. This was also obvious when they were given word problems and investigations. The majority of students were unable to solve problems and they seldom felt confident to even make a start with investigational work.

The researchers discussed the problem and formulated an action plan. An analysis of the National Curriculum and the Key Stage 3 mathematics tests suggested that students needed problem-solving skills and processes to tackle their mathematics work more effectively. The project was set up.

INTERVENTION

Preparations for the intervention programme started with an extensive literature search on problem-solving. The researchers sought to find all recent and relevant literature on problem-solving and its possible influence on mathematics learning. Resources on problem-solving, mainly consisting of tasks with detailed notes and justifications for their use, were bought. After four weeks of discussion and deliberation the four teacher-researchers selected 20 activities to be used in mathematics sessions over two terms. They met once a fortnight to share their perceptions and the data gathered from the sessions. The information collected was also shared with two other mathematics tutors. Some changes were made to the type of resources used and the times of the session as a result of discussions.

DATA COLLECTION

Data collection was discussed with the supervisor from the university. The following sets of data were collected:

- a short questionnaire before the intervention started with four questions seeking students' attitudes to mathematics, their views of their own abilities and their perception of what mathematics was all about;

- a pre-test consisting of questions based on routine skills and problem-solving tasks;

- researchers' logs to record significant incidents and events during the problem-solving sessions – comments on individual students were to be included;

- a post-programme questionnaire using the same questionnaire issued prior to the start of the programme;

- a post-test using similar items to those used in the pre-test.

All the data were analysed by the four teachers, collectively. The findings were shared with the head of the department of mathematics and the university supervisor. A workshop was planned to disseminate the findings of the project.

THE IMPACT

At the start of the project:

- Pupil participation in mathematics sessions was minimal in terms of discussion.

- Their contribution only increased at a very slow pace.

- Students' views of mathematics showed that they perceived the subject as useful and consisting of sums.

- The intervention programme increased students' participation in discussions.

- Increased confidence was recorded in the case of approximately 25 per cent of the students.

- Students made a quicker start with problem-solving situations, compared to their pre-project reluctance and disinterest.

- There was an increase in the mathematics scores of 23 per cent of students.

RESEARCHERS' VIEWS

- Researchers felt that a longer period of intervention may have produced better results in terms of increased confidence and achievement.

- Lower ability students made more progress; this trend was the same across the four classes. This aspect needed further investigation and analysis.

- The researchers felt that they needed to further analyse the content and processes presented through the commercially produced problem-solving materials, with particular reference to their evaluation of the level of improvement in the students' results. Specifically, the question of a match between the skills and the process as required for the tests needed further investigation.

- There was a noticeable shortage of research literature on problem-solving in the UK.

- The participant researchers felt that they were greatly enriched through their experience. The sustained collaborative work and reflection, they felt, were necessary ingredients of their professional development.

I hope you have compiled your own 'action list', including the necessary preparations that one needs to make prior to the start of the project described above. Now compare your list with the list constructed by the researchers given below. The purpose of this exercise is perhaps self-evident. I am trying to highlight the importance of planning in advance and anticipating the outcomes and difficulties when you are carrying out action research.

The 'do' list for the problem-solving project and related notes

- Evidence of lower achievement in mathematics. Where does it come from? Compared to what? Collect and compare school results with the results nationally, in the local education authority and neighbouring schools.

- What are specific problem-solving skills? Find out. Look at documents such as the National Curriculum and analyse national tests. Ask the University tutor to suggest readings. Do a web search for ideas.

- Make a list of specific aims.

- Draw up a timescale.

- Let parents and children know about the project.

- Establish what data are needed and what is feasible.

- Discuss an observation schedule and establish guidelines for consistency between researchers.

- Organise dates for meetings – of researchers, with colleagues and supervisor.

- Create a filing system for storing children's written work.

- Video record sessions?

- Order problem-solving resources (check with local mathematics adviser).

- Recruit two willing colleagues to provide critical feedback every two weeks.

- Design pre- and post-questionnaires and pilot first.

- Organise pre-tests.

- Discuss the format of personal logs of researchers.

- Think about the dissemination of the project. List some ideas.

Although I acknowledge that action lists are always personal to the researcher or to a group of researchers, there are some features of the above list which make it a useful model to consider. Here are my reasons:

- The list is comprehensive and gives attention to detail. The time spent on planning activities is worthwhile, as it will help the smooth running of the project.

- The researchers are led to understand the need for establishing a set of specific aims.

- The plan is very detailed and pays attention to practical aspects such as the storing of students' work and decisions relating to possible formats of the personal logs of the researchers.

- The researchers acknowledge the need for enhancing their own understanding of the topic of study. For example, they aim to seek further clarification of what is meant by problem-solving skills and plan to consult documents and search for relevant readings.

- The need for a baseline is highlighted at the outset.

- The researchers intend to involve others – colleagues, the local adviser, university tutor and criticial friends – to provide feedback.

- They consider what data is needed and how the evidence may be collected at the start.

- It is quite a good idea to consider the dissemination of outcomes at the outset, as it helps you to decide what to collect and the nature of evidence needed.

- It is advisable to let participating students and parents know about the project. You want to avoid them being told about the project by others, which may lead to anxiety and confusion. This is an ethical issue which is discussed in Chapter 5.

FACILITATING AN ACTION PLAN

The role of a supporting mentor or supervisor is of vital importance to an action researcher. In the following section, I have presented a few transcripts of some of my tutorials with a Master's student. Ian is a secondary teacher who was studying for a Master's degree. After completing all the required taught modules he was preparing to carry out his research for his dissertation. Although he subsequently finished his dissertation, which was of very high quality, at the initial stages he was quite often uncertain about what he was doing and how he could manage it all. As part of my preparations for writing this book, I asked Ian if I could tape-record our tutorial sessions and he agreed. The purpose of including these examples is to reinforce the ideas I have highlighted earlier. Ian maintained that the tutorials helped him to focus on his topic and the methodology. You may identify with Ian's experiences which should encourage you to reflect on some of the issues I have discussed earlier. I acknowledge my gratitude to Ian for letting me tape-record our conversations and allowing me to share it with the readers.

Tutorial 1

During this tutorial the following conversation took place.

Ian: I am at the stage of starting to think about my dissertation. I have a vague idea what I want to do. That is it really, I haven't thought about it any further. All I know for certain is that I need to get the work done in six months and write up within four months after that.

VK: What is the topic you are interested in?

Ian: Something on questioning skills.

VK: What about questioning skills? Tell me more.

Ian: Well, I got interested after our assessment lecture on differentiation. Bloom's taxonomy had an impact on my thinking. It is great. I want to do something relating to that as my topic.

VK: What aspect of Bloom's taxonomy interested you the most?

Ian: I was rather hoping you would tell me what to do and how to do it.

VK: Let us start again. You said you were fascinated by the taxonomy, so you tell me what made you so interested.

Ian: The clarity of how the degree of cognitive demand increases when you move on to the higher levels.

VK: Yes, go on.

Ian: I also thought it is a great framework for a teacher to follow. I am sure most of us use the first few levels of the taxonomy in our teaching and never move onto the higher levels of thinking.

VK: Is that one of the areas that impressed you?

Ian: Yes, I think I will do my project based on the application of Bloom's taxonomy in my lesson planning with reference to questioning.

VK: Now you have an idea to develop, the next step is…

Ian: What I would really like you to do, if that is OK, is to give me one or two tasks to do before I see you again.

VK: Well, how about these tasks. Try and write down a working title for your project, it does not have to be final. Second, write half a page of A4 explaining why you wish to undertake the study. You can include an explanation of how you got interested and what motivated you. The third task, write down what Bloom's taxonomy means to you, in your own words.

Tutorial 2

Ian sent me his attempts at the tasks before our next tutorial. During the second tutorial we discussed different directions for the study and Ian decided to select the title: 'Applying Bloom's taxonomy in my teaching'.

VK: What do you mean by applying? What do you intend to do?

Ian: I see what you mean.

After more discussion, Ian decided on a changed title: 'An investigation into possible changes in children's responses, when they are asked questions from the higher levels of the taxonomy'.

Ian: My hunch is that children's answers to questions which test knowledge or comprehension will be quite brief and the questions which involve analysis and evaluation will be fuller and possibly more interesting and demonstrate more thinking.

VK: Is that what you are going to find out?

(Ian had brought a box file, which contained his lecture notes on Bloom's taxonomy and abstracts of two research papers on the topic. He wanted me to set him some more tasks.)

VK: Try and get hold of these two or three books [from a list given during the meeting] and read the relevant sections. Try a web search for any international studies which investigate similar ideas to yours. Bring your nearly final title and a summary of what you have read to the next meeting. Try and put an action plan together for us to look at.

I also encouraged Ian to look at some studies of other Master's students in the library which have been bound and were on display.

Tutorial 3

Ian was happier with the new, focused title and brought an action plan which included the following.

- Read three research papers and the lecture notes again before deciding on the nature of the questions to be used.

- Read about action research as a methodology and jot down why you have selected this as a method to conduct the study. (See notes from research methods lecture.) Include a reference to the participatory nature of action research.

- Focus on three lessons in a week. Possibly from one single subject so that other variables are not introduced.

- Write down a set of questions from the different levels of the taxonomy in the lesson plans.

- Arrange video taping of one session per week for six weeks. Think about what else can be collected as evidence.

- Organise two colleagues to watch the video and make independent comments.

- Make any necessary changes after three weeks.

- A timescale for the fieldwork.

The purpose of including these transcripts is to highlight a few issues which could be useful to readers who may feel some anxiety at the start of their project. It is quite common for a new researcher to select a topic based on a new experience or a new idea which has sparked off an interest. It is likely that the initial title would reflect a wish to take on the topic in its entirety – this may be unrealistic and unmanageable. On many occasions you may have only a vague idea about your research topic, but there is no need to feel guilty about that. Most of my students find it very useful to talk their ideas through with their supervisors and also with colleagues in teaching sessions. Many of them also appreciate being given structured tasks between tutorials.

Having discussed the importance of forward planning and attention to detail, it is time for you to think a little more about what I have discussed previously. Below I will present two research reports to facilitate further consideration of the issues discussed earlier. The first is a report of a study I supervised. The second is from a case study of a project published by the Teacher Training Agency in 1997. The two studies are very different in many respects, as you will see.

First, here is another task: have a look at the title and make a note of what planning needs to be done before the start of the project. After making your list, read the rest of the report.

CASE STUDY 1

Developing speaking skills of pupils for whom English is an Additional Language through playing board games

Aims

- To design a set of board games which will encourage children to engage in more speaking.

- To investigate whether teachers can improve the speaking skills of Year 2 children for whom English is an Additional Language (EAL pupils), by engaging them in specially designed board games.

CONTINUED

What was the study about?

This study investigated the effects of using specially designed board games on the development of speaking skills of 16 pupils in a Year 2 class over a six-month period. The research was carried out by the literacy coordinator with support from the local education authority literacy consultant and the local adviser for children for whom English is an Additional Language.

Summary of findings

- In most cases, pupils (11 out of 16) showed considerable improvement in their speaking skills as a result of playing specially designed board games.

- Initially, pupils were reluctant to participate in the board games. They felt that their lack of ability to speak fluently would be a barrier to winning the games.

- The quality of children's talk improved during the intervention programme.

- The project provided opportunities for involving parents and carers in the development of the children's spoken language.

- Parents who were involved in the project commented that their own language skills had improved as a result of the project and they felt better able to support their children's learning at home.

Background

This research project was located in a multicultural infant school with 212 pupils. For 63 per cent of the children English is an Additional Language. The aim of the study was to raise the children's achievement. In this particular project development of children's speaking skills was targeted, as it was hypothesised that their lack of speaking skills may affect their writing skills. The children who participated in the project were all well behaved but seemed to lack confidence in participating in class discussions. This lack of confidence may have been the result of their inability to speak

CONTINUED

English fluently. An intervention programme of using games was planned for two reasons. First, children are generally quite motivated to participate in games and, second, playing board games would involve working in groups, thus generating the need for talk as a means of communication.

Specific objectives

The project was set up to:

- investigate what contributes to the development of speaking skills. This would be achieved through reading literature and by consultations with experts;

- establish the level of speaking skills of EAL children prior to the project. This would provide a basis for monitoring;

- design a set of ten board games which will encourage the use of the English language;

- encourage children's parents to participate in the project by sending copies of the board games home, with instructions in both English and the language spoken at home;

- monitor any changes in the children's development of vocabulary, their fluency of speech, their reading skills and their level of confidence;

- assess whether the programme had any effect on the children's writing skills;

- disseminate the findings and ideas for the resources to colleagues and other local schools.

Gathering data

A number of methods was used. The project was set within a qualitative paradigm. As it involved a small sample, the use of quantitative data could not be justified. However, evidence of changes in scores was recorded numerically. The following information was collected:

- baseline test results;

CONTINUED

- samples of children's writing throughout the period of the project;

- tape recordings of group activity throughout the project to gauge the level of participation;

- researcher's diary of significant events;

- copies of board games and a list of anticipated learning outcomes resulting from their use;

- the attendance of pupils.

Design of the board games

The board games were designed by the researcher, taking into account research findings on the development of speaking skills. The support staff actually made them. Instructions were word-processed. Multiple copies of the games and instructions were made available for children to take home.

The intervention programme

Parents were informed of the project before the start. Children were involved in the games session four times a week for approximately one hour. At each session, data was collected by the researcher and validated through discussions with the local advisers. The advisers were also involved in analysing the data.

Results

- There was an increased level of confidence in the children's speaking skills as evidenced by their readiness to speak and the spontaneity of their responses. Indicators of increased participation were also noted. The children's reluctance to go out at playtime, so that they could continue to play the games, was quite common.

- The number of English words used in the session increased steadily throughout the period of the project.

- Parents also showed a high level of commitment to the programme. They were actively involved and very enthusiastic for their children to bring the games for homework and they always

CONTINUED

played with their children. One parent commented on the board games taking over from *television time*.

- There was a marked improvement in the quality of the children's writing.

- There was, however, no marked improvement in children's reading skills.

- The research team was invited by a national publisher to help develop a set of board games in both Mathematics and English, specifically designed for EAL children.

Endnote

The project was worthwhile in terms of the enhancement of children's literacy skills, and speaking skills in particular. As there was no control group, it cannot be claimed without qualification that it was the intervention programme that produced such positive results. Using a control group was beyond the scope of this project. One certain, beneficial aspect of the project was the learning processes it offered to the researcher. At the start of the programme, the researcher was frustrated and helpless and wishing to take some positive steps towards helping her EAL children to participate more in the lessons. The outcome of the project was pleasing in that it achieved its aims. The researcher's own knowledge of teaching EAL children was enhanced through her own reading and by her 'living' the project over a sustained period.

Compared with the first case study, there are several new features in Case Study 2 opposite. First, it involves a whole institution and a much larger sample. It also uses numerical data. The study can still be described as action research. I decided to include the report in its entirety because it demonstrates most of the ingredients which make action research a desirable, productive and innovative methodology. The study involves collaboration, meticulous planning and rigorous analysis leading to remarkable application.

This report is reproduced by the kind permission of the Teacher Training Agency (1997). References and figures were provided within the original text which are not included here.

CASE STUDY 2

The role of handwriting in raising achievement

Research carried out by Donna Barratt and Sue Wheatley, Yeading Junior School, Hayes, Middlesex.

Aim

To establish whether fluent handwriting can be a factor in raising achievement.

Dimensions of this case study

The study surveyed the handwriting characteristics of 1,192 students across the 11–16 age range in a large comprehensive school.

Summary of findings for this case study

- Handwriting speed was a factor in student achievement, regardless of ability.

- Students achieving higher-than-expected GCSE English language grades tended to write at a higher speed than those who underachieved (expectation and achievement being related to Year 7 CATS ability tests).

- At all ability levels students who achieved higher-than-expected GCSE grades had a better handwriting style than those who underachieved. Although this study does not offer evidence of cause and effect, the evidence suggested that handwriting quality and quantity are strongly associated with examination achievement at all but the very highest levels of ability.

- Slow handwriters had problems with poor motor coordination, spellings, letter formation, word shape and discrimination between upper and lower case.

CONTINUED

- Over 40 per cent of students in Year 7, reducing only to 20 per cent in Year 11, were writing slowly. Of these, some had great difficulty making what they wrote legible.

- Boys in Year 7 wrote more slowly than girls but increased their speed each year. By year 11 they were slightly faster than girls. Girls' writing speed increased from Year 7 to Year 8, then stayed constant.

- There was a correlation between speed and Reading/Spelling age in Year 7 for boys and girls. An increase in speed of 3–4 w.p.m. corresponded on average to an increase in Reading/Spelling age 3–4 months.

- Boys had a higher frequency of handwriting problems than girls. Failure to join up letters was the problem with the greatest incidence in boys and girls, although overall it was at a higher level in girls. There was no clear link between the frequency of letter joining as a characteristic and handwriting speed. Hence 'printing' does not necessarily limit handwriting speed.

- The effect of joins is different for boys and girls. For boys, failure to join up correctly is associated with an average drop of half a grade in GCSE English. For girls it is associated with an average drop of a whole grade.

Background

Current approaches to literacy emphasise reading and spelling with relatively little attention given to the role of handwriting. This study suggests that the connection between handwriting and literacy may also be very significant.

The research set out to examine the overall pattern of handwriting speed and legibility in a large secondary comprehensive school. The study was based on the premise that the speed and legibility of handwriting are key factors in a student's capacity to do well at school, particularly in public examinations. A previous study in the school, of students with motor coordination difficulties, had shown that those with severe difficulties were very concerned about the appearance of their work and were under-achieving (Rutherford, 1996). More detailed information about the writing habits of the whole student body was needed to help the school plan effective teaching strategies which would both overcome these particular difficulties and have more general applicability across the school.

The research was also influenced by a recent study of the approach to the teaching of handwriting used in France where, according to Thomas (1997)'... by contrast [to the UK] handwriting, particularly flowing joined-up handwriting, is considered fundamental, a physical skill that, once mastered, unlocks the mind'. In French schools the teaching process begins at age 3 and goes on until the age of 8 or 9. It takes precedence over reading 'because writing is considered more demanding'. Thomas remarks that the results indicate that, 'It is as though, having automated the hand, children's minds are liberated to release their ideas more efficiently and creatively on paper.' If this is the case it seems possible that difficulties with 'automating the hand' could have a negative effect on achievement. Initiatives to overcome motor coordination difficulties might, therefore, through improvements in handwriting, improve literacy and achievement.

The survey

The English faculty carried out the survey during the winter of 1996/97. Our starting point was a very simple search for information about three things: how many students wrote slowly, what the average speed was in each age group, and what pattern we would find over the school as a whole. If an output of 12 words a minute over ten minutes is regarded by educational psychologists as 'slow' what is 'fast'?

CONTINUED

	No. of Students	Below 5	5–9	10–14	15–19	20–24	24–29	30–34	Over 35
Year 7	275	1%	8%	35%	38%	16%	2%	0%	0%
Year 8	175	0%	3%	17%	38%	28%	9%	4%	0%
Year 9	265	0%	5%	17%	37%	27%	10%	3%	0%
Year 10	215	0%	3%	16%	34%	28%	12%	6%	1%
Year 11	262	0%	2%	17%	23%	35%	16%	5%	2%
Total	1,192	4	55	251	404	316	115	39	8
Average		0	5%	21%	34%	27%	10%	3%	1%

Speed of handwriting over ten minutes (free choice of subject matter) in words per minute. Entries are percentages, rounded to whole numbers, and sum to 100 across rows.

Key questions about handwriting

To discover how handwriting can contribute to achievement, we set out to explore the following questions:

● *What is the pattern of handwriting speed in the school as a whole?*

The survey results, illustrated in the table, showed a wide range of writing speed in the school as a whole. The majority in each age group wrote at speeds between 15 and 25 words per minute.

● *How many students produce written work which is challenging to read or illegible?*

Although very few students in the school as a whole produced illegible scripts, many of them showed problems, particularly with joining up.

● *Does the primary school of origin affect handwriting skills?*

There were no systematic differences among children at Year 7. However, in the case of some primary schools, the numbers were too small to be statistically significant.

● *What makes handwriting difficult to read?*

CONTINUED

Poor letter formation, word shape, spelling and confusion of upper/lower case were the main problems identified. These problems increased as students got older and were more common for boys than girls.

● *What makes handwriting a difficult task?*

Although this study did not specifically address the factors which made handwriting difficult, where problems were noted, the scripts also showed signs characteristics of poor motor coordination.

● *Are there any significant age and gender differences in the development of handwriting?*

Speed increases with age. Among younger children, girls write faster than boys but by Year 10 or 11 the boys have caught up. In general, handwriting problems do not decrease with age and some problems, for example word/letter formation, increase with age. More boys exhibit more problems of the kind described in this study than do girls.

● *Is there any correlation between poor handwriting and achievement?*

Among Year 7 students there was a small correlation with CATs scores. At GCSE slow writers perform less well in English Language than faster writers, even after adjusting for ability. Furthermore, the effect of joins is different for boys than for girls. For boys, failure to join up correctly is associated with an average drop of half of a grade. For girls it is associated with an average drop of a whole grade. Results for handwriting and achievement in GCSE Science were similar to those for GCSE English, but the differences were not as pronounced as in the English examination. Disentangling the best predictors of success at GCSE is not straightforward because the different aspects and measures of legibility are interrelated, and because of their different incidences for boys and girls. However, speed still has a small estimated effect on GCSE English grades. This study did not explore the nature of the relationship between spellings and joining, but the findings suggest that further work in this area would repay investigation.

● *Is there a connection between writing speed and legibility?*

There was no general association between speed and legibility except that those that joined up wrote faster. There was a correlation between speed and National Curriculum levels for writing, possibly because 'joining' is an element in the NC levels.

● *What implications will the results of the survey have on our teaching methods?*

These emanate from three sources of information. First, the likelihood that a number of students in each class have writing difficulties means that teachers need to consider the demands they make on the student's ability to write clearly and quickly and need to develop strategies to help them record their work. Secondly, the evidence showing that problems increase with age suggests that students with handwriting problems should receive more attention. Handwriting should be taught throughout the years of secondary education and this may be particularly important for boys. In this respect the findings support the work of Connor (1995) who suggests that '... among boys, there appears still to be scope for maturation and improvement in writing performance from Year 10 onward'. Thirdly, the data show that generally, among students with SEN, a higher proportion are slow writers and have poor handwriting. However, these problems were also identified among those not identified as having SEN. This suggests that handwriting is a general problem among students and is therefore a matter for all teachers, not just SEN specialists.

Ways forward

The implications of this study turned out to be more far reaching than anticipated. Although the questions raised are complex, the message is clear. Continued attention to handwriting throughout the school years is essential and an early start with joined-up writing will aid a process that is far more than purely physical. The survey drew attention to a number of issues:

CONTINUED

For students' written work as a source of reading matter

For students, their work is a prime source of reading matter. Those who are unable to read what they have written cannot gain much satisfaction or improvement from their own key source material. It is in this area that the full significance of the survey is most apparent. If a quarter of the students struggle, for whatever reason, to write fluently and legibly about a subject of their own choice, how do they fare when the subject matter is unfamiliar? The survey results show that most students' handwriting does improve between Years 7 and 11. This suggests that by helping students develop fluent, legible, joined-up handwriting, teachers in secondary schools play a significant role in improving literacy. This has implications for whole school curriculum planning and staff development.

The connection between spelling, handwriting and reading

Multi-sensory approaches to the teaching of literacy suggest that encouraging secondary school students to write legibly and fluently will improve reading and spelling. There are implications, however, in terms of teacher and student time. The findings suggest that the connection between accurate spelling and joined handwriting may be a key element, which therefore needs to be explored in greater detail.

Students with problems of speed or legibility

Students (25 per cent in this study) unable to write faster than 15 words per minute will be struggling in all lessons where a lot of writing is required. Alternative strategies are required to minimise the loss for those who cannot cope with the writing 'input' and 'output' demand of them. If asked to copy from the board, their notes are likely to be illegible and/or unfinished. Furthermore, although the majority of children write at a reasonable speed by the time they reach Year 8, their handwriting is still developing. If asked to write too much, too often, too fast before they have settled to a mature hand, their writing will deteriorate and bad habits become entrenched.

CONTINUED

The writing demand across the curriculum and the age range

Study of the total amount of written work expected of students could lead, for example, to a reduction in writing demand in favour of teaching methods less dependent on written work, or the use of alternatives such as prepared worksheets or IT. There could also be an enhanced role for subjects such as Science, Geography, Technology, Languages and Maths to teach handwriting skills more explicitly in its different registers, for example, scripts suitable for maps and diagrams and numbers. In those lessons where the pressure on writing speed is less severe (Languages, Technology, Science) there could be an expectation that what is written must be of a very high standard. Most students can and should be expected to write their name and address legibly on an envelope. If they can do this they can do other equally short written tasks legibly too. This would have the effect of raising expectations and giving opportunities for practising and improving on previous best. A by-product of helping poor spellers and readers to write well enough to make reading their own work a possibility would be that their notes could be used for revision.

Conclusions

Further research is required to:

- Establish whether the results of this survey are typical.

- Examine the role of Occupational Therapists in helping schools develop preventative strategies for those with motor coordination difficulties. This has implications for schools in, for example, the selection of school furniture, physical education and the creative arts.

- Develop successful whole-school handwriting policies set within a framework which recognises the needs of those with motor coordination difficulties. In view of the lack of attention currently given to the teaching of handwriting in secondary schools, policy development there should be a priority.

CONTINUED

A note on methods

Students were tested using a test normally applied by the school's educational psychologist to assess for GCSE. The students were asked to write freely on a subject of their choice for ten minutes with an extra 2.5 minutes for correction. We received 1,273 scripts, representing about 80 per cent of the total possible. Of these, complete background data was available for 1,192 students. The remaining 20 per cent were accounted for by 7 classes (3 in Year 8) who missed the test. We were aware of the limitations of the test and of the reservations expressed by Sawyer, Gray and Champness (1996) and Alston (1994). Nonetheless it seemed appropriate for our purposes, not least because of its closeness to a simulation of an examination setting. The data which the scripts themselves would yield was also important; words per minute was only one category. Despite reservations, the data turned out to be very rich and raised a number of further questions. Hence the choice of test appears to have suited the research aims.

Data analysis

Readers should refer to our full report for a detailed description of the methodology used in the analysis. Handwriting is notoriously variable and difficult to assess objectively. The criteria chosen for this study were therefore those that could be easily replicated and kept as simple and objective as possible. Note that in the table, no distinction is made between boys and girls or SEN and non-SEN students.

SUMMARY

In this chapter I have stressed the importance of drawing up action plans. The reader wishing to map out a journey through the sequences of tasks demanded by the specific, chosen action research topic is first recommended to focus on an appropriate title. The construction of a 'do list' of action follows. The role of critical friends and colleagues is emphasised, as I believe that the dynamics of collective thinking can create awareness of any shortcomings as well as generate previously unexpected lines of enquiry. Case studies are provided as guided tours through journeys taken by other action researchers. These were presented to enable the readers to acquire a kind of simulated experience of action research before embarking on their own, real journey of enquiry.

Chapter 5

Gathering data

KEY POINTS

This chapter provides guidance on techniques for gathering data. It focuses on:

- ethical considerations;

- a discussion of methodology;

- methods of data collection.

INTRODUCTION

When you set up an action plan for your action research, you will have given some consideration to an all important part of conducting any research – gathering data. You would probably have been asking yourself a question for some time: what methods will I be using and how will I go about organising the collection of data? This chapter is devoted to aspects relating to data-gathering. As I mentioned in Chapter 4, as preparation for writing this book, I kept tape-recordings of some of my tutorials with students and practitioners who wished to adopt action research as the methodology for their research. I start this chapter with a transcript of one such conversation. Martina, studying for a Master's programme, was intending to carry out a project on curriculum differentiation. After the first few tutorials, she decided to narrow the focus of the study to investigate how four class teachers of Year 5 children addressed curriculum differentiation in their classrooms.

⬤⬤⬤ Our conversation

Martina: I am now ready to start collecting data. I have got some ideas. First, my worry is that I am only working with just four teachers. Is that a big enough sample?

VK: Big enough sample for what?

Martina: Big enough to have any credibility when I write it up.

VK: Why do you have such doubt?

Martina: I thought you had to collect information from a larger sample for any research.

VK: Let us go back a bit. What is the purpose of your research – of course, other than the fact that it is part of your study? What are your aims?

Martina: To find out how different teachers deal with differentiation and learn from it. I will compare what I find out from other classrooms with what happens in my classroom. I need to think carefully about what I am doing and get some practical ideas because my head teacher wants me to design a policy on curricuculum differentiation.

We then talked about the timescale Martina had to complete the project in terms of the requirements set by her institution and her study for accreditation purposes. We discussed the nature of action research, which offers scope for a small-scale, focused study on aspects of practice. We agreed that the purpose of her research was not to make any generalisations about curriculum differentiation in the whole country, but to study a snapshot of what happens in her school with a small number of teachers involved. Personal theorising of principles through participatory research was the main purpose of Martina undertaking her study. Then we went on to discuss what kinds of data she needed to collect.

In the following sections, I will present a variety of data-gathering methods, their relative merits and possible disadvantages for use in action research. The ultimate decision of what kind of data you need and what methods to use will depend on:

- the nature of the evidence you need to collect;

- the timescale for the study;

- the time available to you for carrying out the project;

- the usefulness of the data you intend to collect;

- a consideration of how you may interpret the data.

Using several different methods for collecting data does not make your study any better; I would say that it is the quality of your data that matters. A set of data which has no depth is not going to prove useful when the time comes for data analysis and drawing conclusions. Keep reminding yourself that you will need to analyse the data you collect and provide supporting evidence from the data to justify your conclusions.

Your readings would have provided you with some insights into what aspects you are looking for. In Martina's case, she decided to focus on using four methods of data collection: interviewing class teachers on their perceptions of how they achieved differentiation in lessons; collecting lesson plans from all the teachers involved; observing their lessons; and collecting students' written work. Martina was encouraged to consider some of the aspects she was looking for and how she needed to plan for unexpected outcomes. Running a pilot study was suggested to her so that she could consider how she was going to organise her data. She and I discussed when she was going to collect her data and looked into the practical aspects of school timetables and cover. Did she need to prepare any special resources? Did she have permission from the teachers she was going to study? Had she considered how she was going to share her perceptions and observations with the four teachers? Martina also decided to ask two of her colleagues, teaching a different year group, to act as her critical friends.

ETHICAL CONSIDERATIONS

When you are carrying out research it is important to follow ethical guidelines. Academic institutions should have a set of guidelines for their students to follow. Reading the guidelines on ethics published by the British Education Research Association (BERA – see the section on

Useful websites at the end of the book) is a useful starting point. Following strict guidelines on ethical issues is of particular importance for action researchers because of the small-scale nature of the projects located within the working situations of the researchers. Special care needs to be taken both for data collection and the dissemination of findings as it would be easy to recognise people and events within local situations. You may find the following guidance helpful.

● Always obtain permission from the participants. If you are collecting data about children, their parents need to be informed. The same principle applies to colleagues, members of local education authorities, parents and governors.

● Provide a copy of your set of ethical guidelines to the participants.

● Explain the purpose of the research. In action research the outcomes are most likely to be used for improving aspects of practice and, therefore, there is less likelihood of resistance from participants.

● Keep real names and the identities of subjects confidential and unrecognisable.

● Share information with colleagues and others whose responses you are interpreting so that they can verify the relevancy and accuracy of what you are reporting.

● If you are intending to introduce new ideas and set up interventions with pupils, their parents need to be told.

● Be sensitive to the feelings and perceptions of both parents and students. This is particularly important if the intervention programme is designed to improve aspects of education, as the students being targeted may be seen to be at an advantage. You need to make it clear that the findings of a research experiment would benefit all.

● Be as non-intrusive as possible in your data collection.

● When you are researching socially sensitive issues, you need to make extra efforts to share your purpose and objectives with the participants.

A CHECKLIST

You may find the following checklist useful before you start collecting information for your project.

- Are ethical issues being considered?

- Have you got permission from all those who are involved in the project such as parents, colleagues and the head teacher?

- Have you checked all the equipment you would need to use? Are the tape recorders, video recorders and cameras working?

- Have you considered how you would validate the information for accuracy and relevance?

- Where will you store the information?

- Have you a general idea how you may interpret the data?

- Have you organised the resources you need, including any costs?

DISCUSSION OF METHODOLOGY

If you are carrying out your research as part of obtaining a qualification, you will certainly need to demonstrate some knowledge of different research paradigms. An elaborate discussion of different paradigms of research is beyond the scope of this book, so if your study leads to a dissertation you will need to do supplementary reading which should have been provided in your research methods lectures. But I think it is useful for all researchers to have some basic understanding of the different types of research.

Researchers often refer to *positivist* and *naturalistic* paradigms. A positivist researcher often gathers large amounts of data in the form of large-scale surveys and analyses them in order to make generalizations, while a naturalistic, interpretative researcher tries to get inside individuals and institutions to understand situations and people. As an action researcher you are likely to follow the latter method.

An action researcher may use a variety of methods to collect data. Ask yourself the following questions before you start collecting your data:

- What are the aims of my research?

- What aspects am I focusing on?

● What do I need as evidence to achieve my aims?

● What is realistic and feasible?

● How should I record the data?

QUALITATIVE OR QUANTITATIVE DATA

Action researchers should also be aware of the two categories of data – quantitative and qualitative – and consider their usefulness within the context of their work. Quantitative data can be measured and represented by numbers. When a researcher handles large amounts of data – for example a large number of questionnaires, surveys, tests results – it is often necessary to analyse them using statistical methods and present them in the form of tables and charts. If you are collecting views using questionnaires from a small group of children or colleagues about their perceptions of a style of teaching or attitudes, you may want to represent the data numerically using tables and charts. The use of questionnaires within a qualitative study often provides ideas for further exploration. But it is likely that an action researcher would predominantly be working within a qualitative paradigm as the data may be more in the form of transcripts, descriptions and documents for analysis. It must be stressed that qualitative data is not inferior in status and, in action research, it can illuminate human feelings and provide rich insights into actions and their consequences. What is important is to select the type of data which will serve the purpose of your study. If you are undertaking action research for the purpose of obtaining a qualification, it is well worth including the distinction between quantitative and qualitative paradigms in order to demonstrate your understanding of research methodology and to provide a justification for the methods you have selected for data collection.

METHODS OF DATA COLLECTION

In the following section, we will look at some commonly used methods for data collection. Data collection methods are also referred to as methods of instrumentation. Before exploring the different methods, let me provide you with two important points which all researchers could usefully bear in mind when planning their data collection.

- There are many ways of gathering data; you have to choose the most suitable method for the task in hand.

- It is the quality of the data you collect that is more important than the number of ways you collect data.

The methods described in the following sections are:

- using questionnaires;

- conducting interviews;

- gathering documentary evidence;

- field diaries and notes;

- systematic observation.

For each method of data-gathering, I have tried to provide some general guidance as well as indicate some advantages and any possible disadvantages for that particular method. Some examples are given in sections which I felt needed exemplification.

USING QUESTIONNAIRES

The use of questionnaires at the start of a project can often be very useful because it helps you to collect a range of information with relative ease, which can then be followed up as necessary. For example, if you are carrying out a study on how an intervention programme may help to change student attitudes to mathematics, the use of a questionnaire provides you with a simple means to collect information on student attitudes before any intervention takes place. The completed questionnaires can help in two ways. They provide baseline data on student attitudes before the intervention begins. Secondly, an analysis of the questionnaires may help to shape the nature of the questions you may want to ask during any personal interviews or observations you may wish to conduct. Within a questionnaire, you can use both short questions and open-ended questions which need fuller responses. When working with children, I often find they enjoy the experience of completing the questionnaires so they can be encouraged to provide full information in response to questions.

Guidelines

Here is a set of guidelines you should find useful to consider:

- Keep the questionnaire simple. By designing appropriate questions, you can often gather a decent amount of data by using a small number of questions.

- Consider how you may analyse the responses to the questions at the time of design.

- Start with questions about the factual information required.

- Use simple language which the respondents will understand.

- Questions which have discrete responses such as 'How much do you enjoy PE lessons?' with options such as *a lot, not at all* or *sometimes*, are easier to interpret and represent as charts and tables for easy reference.

- Open-ended questions are useful, but give some thought to how you would analyse them.

- Avoid leading questions. For example, a question such as 'Which part of the lesson did you enjoy the most?' assumes that the student enjoyed some parts of a lesson, which may not necessarily be the case.

- Emphasise the anonymity of the responses as children and adults are often sensitive to who else may be told about how they have responded.

- Do a pilot run before you give out questionnaires and make adjustments as necessary. Acknowledge, in your final report, your pilot effort and any changes that were made to the final version of the questionnaire.

- Questions do not always have to use words. For example, I have seen some effective use of pictures of happy, puzzled or sad faces, with younger children being asked to select a picture in response to questions such as: 'How do you feel when you are asked to answer a mental maths question during a carpet session?'

- Take account of the reading ability of students when administering a questionnaire.

Advantages of using questionnaires

Questionnaires

- enable you to collect background and baseline information quite easily;

- can help you to gather a reasonable amount of data in a short time;

- provide information which can be followed up;

- provide a format making it easy to represent information;

- are suitable for collecting initial information on attitudes and perceptions.

Disadvantages of using questionnaires

- You may be subjective and introduce bias in the type of questions you ask.

- Responses to questions may be influenced by what the respondents believe you want to hear.

- Designing a questionnaire needs great skill, especially when you use open-ended questions which are designed to be probing.

- If you are using questionnaires in order to collect data from a large group of people who are not within your institution, returns and response rates may be too low to ensure a valid research outcome.

An example of a questionnaire

As part of her data-gathering activities Stephanie, a member of the senior management team in her school, decided to use a questionnaire to collect information about students' interests, aptitudes and aspirations, prior to designing an intervention programme to be delivered after school to bright students who had the potential to go to university. This was considered, by Stephanie, within the context of the government's Widening Participation strategy. The extracts given on page 90 are taken from Stephanie's questionnaire.

The purpose of this questionnaire is to help you to think about your interests which you may like to pursue or develop. It will also help me to organise some out-of-school activities for you. The information you give in the questionnaire is confidential and will not be shared with anyone else, unless you wish me to do so.

For some of the questions you are asked to provide brief answers and, for other questions, you are invited to give more information.

1. **Imagine you are one of a group of students who won a prize in school to set up an exhibition. What role would you want to take?**

    A. Organiser
    B. Artist
    C. Writing and designing brochures for publicity
    D. Be in charge of sound effects
    E. Any other (say which, and explain why):

    ....

    ....

    ....

2. **Suppose a publisher approached you and asked you to help an author write a students' book on one of the following subjects. Which of these will you choose?**

    A. Science
    B. Mathematics
    C. History
    D. Social issues
    E. Art
    F. Technology
    G. Other:

    ....

    ....

    ....

3. **If you could select from the following club activities after school, which would you choose?**

   A. A sports activity
   B. Creative writing
   C. Learn a new language
   D. Web design
   E. Learn to play a new instrument
   F. A different club activity that you would like to see in the list. Say which:

   ....

   ....

   ....

4. **What do you expect to be doing in ten years' time?**

   ....

   ....

   ....

5. **What do you think you should do between now and ten years' time to achieve what you want to be?**

   ....

   ....

   ....

Students' responses to the questionnaire proved useful to Stephanie. Her own evaluation of the use of the questionnaire was as follows:

I used about ten multiple choice questions at the start, which the students could respond to quite quickly. As there were about 120 students taking part in the project I was pleased to be able to collect a good amount of information without much effort. The analysis was simple, as I could classify the responses into numbers and represent them visually, using tables and graphs. I felt that the open-ended questions were necessary to encourage students to reveal their aspirations and expectations without giving them predetermined options to choose from.

Responses to the open-ended questions involved greater effort when it came to analysing them. Nevertheless, these questions provided answers relating to some of the aspects I needed to explore. I needed to find out the kind of aspirations the students had and their perceptions of how they would be able to achieve them. Analysis of these types of questions revealed some significant information. For example, only 14 students expressed any desire to pursue an academic career and listed university education in their future plans. It was also very useful to note that a large number of students had dreams about becoming successful pop singers or sports personalities. In general, the questionnaire provided much useful data which helped me to design an intervention programme. I selected a sub-sample of students to interview in order to gather more information. I did refine the questions after a pilot run, but it was worth the effort because the questionnaires enabled me to collect much useful data within a short time.

CONDUCTING INTERVIEWS

The main purpose of conducting interviews is to gather responses which are richer and more informative than questionnaire data. In some cases, adults and children give more honest responses in a one-to-one situation. As it is impossible to take notes on all that is said during an interview, I recommend tape-recording the interview. Then, either you can later listen to the tapes or read a fully transcribed version of the interviews when you wish to analyse them. Tape-recording also makes it possible for the researcher to give full attention to the context of the interview.

Some guidelines

- Select comfortable surroundings for the interview.

- Make sure that the interviews are not too long. About half an hour to 40 minutes is about right.

- Have some idea about what you want to ask. This will, of course, depend on the research topic and what aspects you are investigating. Semi-structured interviews allow you to probe further during the interview.

- If you intend to ask factual questions start with them.

- Start with a simple question.

- Explain the purpose of the interview in a positive way. I often start with: 'I need your help to find out more about ...' Or, 'I am working on a project to write something about how children ... and what you are going to tell me will certainly help'.

- Ensure anonymity so that the interviewee feels relaxed.

- Try not to convey your opinions at the interview.

- Avoid leading questions such as: 'When I asked you what 5 and 5 makes, did you use your fingers?', 'Spellings are easy for you, are they not?'

- Use open-ended questions. Questions which start, for example, with 'What is your ...', 'Who is ...' or 'Do you like history?' do provide you with information, but useful ways of gathering fuller and richer answers would be to ask questions in the form: 'That is interesting. Tell me more', 'How would you explain it to someone who does not know anything about it?'

- Sometimes it is fruitful to interview a group of children together. It is very important to keep children focused during group interviews.

- Always review responses to interviews and refine procedures and questions if necessary.

Advantages of carrying out interviews

- Interview transcripts provide powerful evidence for presenting data and making conclusions.

- Interviews can provide a relaxed context for exploration.

- The interviewer can steer the discussion through a fruitful route.

- Group interviews save time and are realistic in classroom contexts.

- Interviews can provide unexpected but useful perspectives.

Disadvantages

- Conducting interviews is more time-consuming than using questionnaires.

● Typing transcripts requires a good amount of time.

● Interviewing may not always be a suitable method for use with children who are not confident speakers and those with language problems.

● The use of tape recorders may intimidate some students.

A sample interview

Stephanie, whose questionnaire was discussed in the previous section, interviewed a sub-sample of students after they completed their questionnaires. The following interview with Guli was revealing:

Stephanie: I see you have written here that you would like to see yourself as working in the City earning a lot of money. Tell me more about it.

Guli: I mean a lawyer or something like that. They earn a lot of money and do an interesting job.

S: What would you find interesting about a lawyer's job?

G: All sorts of things. Now let me think … [pause]

S: No rush, do think about it before you tell me …

G: I like watching lawyers on television. They have to really think hard about how to argue a case even when they know their clients are guilty. That takes some work. I also like the way they have to stand up and argue point by point. It looks as though they are really enjoying their job.

S: Anything else that appeals to you?

G: Yes, they all dress so smart and have posh cars.

S: Do you think you will become a lawyer?

G: I would like to, but it is hard. My mum wouldn't know how to go about it. You would have to go to university, won't you? My mum can't spell the word university let alone send me to one…

The second transcript is an interview with Lloyd:

Stephanie: You have said you want to earn a million pounds as a footballer. Do you think you will make it?

Lloyd: It is a dream really. It doesn't matter if it happens or not, does it?

S: I am just interested to know how you would go about achieving your dream. For example, tell me why you think you could become a successful footballer.

L: Because I want to be one.

S: Do you play football?

L: A bit on Saturdays.

S: Would you say you are good at football?

L: I am all right. I suppose you are thinking … [pause] … you are thinking … I am not good enough to become a rich footballer. I suppose you will be right. Only very few people can really become millionaire footballers … There is no harm in dreaming though …

Stephanie wrote about her interviews:

It really was very revealing. Guli is a very bright girl, but I had no idea that she and her family would need support to consider an academic route for her. There were other students I interviewed who also showed similar needs. I am happy to say that this information helped me in two ways. First, it highlighted the need for organising some parents' sessions in which to talk to them about career choices and educational requirements; this could became part of my intervention programme. It also provided a baseline for Guli at the start of the programme which enabled me to track her progress. In Lloyd's case, it occurred to me that even during my interview he started questioning the nature of his ambition and viewed it as an impossibility. It made me think that as part of our intervention programme it would be useful for students to be encouraged to think about the feasibility of their ambitions.

GATHERING DOCUMENTARY EVIDENCE

In some cases your data collection would include studying documentary evidence such as policies, minutes of meetings, teachers' planning records and students' work. These sources can often provide a useful background and context for the project and also can be very illuminating, especially when you are comparing what is claimed and what has happened in practice. One of my students, looking for evidence on differentiation, found several claims about differentiation in the school policy, but little evidence of it in practice within curriculum plans or the actual teaching which she observed. Documents can often provide relevant evidence and are very useful for constructing the whole picture. I have seen students using curriculum planning records over a period of time and keeping an ongoing record of any changes. Similarly, students' written work and portfolios can help the researcher to note progress over time. Photographs capturing critical moments and products are also useful as evidence. This is particularly helpful in early years classrooms.

Advantages of gathering documentary evidence

- Documentary evidence can provide insights into a situation where research takes place.

- In most cases it provides information without much effort.

- A record of objectives and policies which are not easily communicated can be accessed through documents.

- It can support other forms of evidence collected.

Disadvantages

- Trust in the researcher will be necessary before documents are given.

- As it may constitute large amounts of data, analysis could be difficult.

- Personal choices may affect the type of documents collected.

FIELD DIARIES AND NOTES

The use of a research diary, or field notes as they are sometime referred to, is often very helpful and this device is becoming more popular with my students. It is used for keeping a record of what happens, of why and where your ideas evolved and of the research process itself. Of course, your research dairy could be extremely valuable when it comes to writing up your project. The reflective process involved in writing a diary contributes to the professional development of the researcher. Diary entries need not be very long. You could record significant events during your observations or particular situations and your feelings.

Guidelines

- A free writing style can be employed when keeping field notes and diaries.

- It is useful to have a structure in your mind. Within that structure, you need to have the flexibility to make notes about aspects which may not fit into your predetermined structure, although they are significant to you.

- Reflective writing supports professional development. Try to be analytical and reflective in your entries.

- Including a section for personal commentary supports analysis and discussion at a later stage.

Advantages of keeping research diaries

- Keeping a research diary helps to personalise your project. This is important in an action research project as the main purpose is to make changes in practice.

- Diaries help to keep a progress check on the project.

- Field diaries often supplement information obtained from other sources.

- The process of reflective writing is an integral part of professional development.

● The contents of a diary should help you to construct your research story as a case study.

● Disadvantages

It is difficult to think of disadvantages of keeping a personal journal of incidents during an action research project. However, the following aspects may be worth considering:

● A researcher may be tempted to write too much, which can lead to difficulties at the time of analysis.

● It is sometimes difficult to keep up the writing regularly.

● When the research is not going according to plan, there may be a tendency to stop writing.

● Personalising the incidents may lead to subjectivity.

● SYSTEMATIC OBSERVATION

Observation plays an important part in any kind of data-gathering and most action research projects use this as an instrument. Observation is a natural process – we observe people and incidents all the time and based on the observations, we make judgements. Basically, we are making use of this method within the research process where there is a need for more systematic observation, so that the information we collect can be used for the purpose of the study being carried out.

When we consider observation as a method for data collection, two types of observations are often referred to – participant and non-participant observation. Participant observation involves the researcher living in the context and being a part of it, but one needs to be aware of what Cohen and Manion (1994) point out, that there is a danger of being too subjective in data collection and this can introduce bias. One also needs to be conscious of this and acknowledge, at the outset, the possibility of introducing what one wishes to see into the data gathered. We must also try not to distort the interpretations. Non-participant observation is less subjective. The latter involves observing actions and interactions, perhaps sitting in a corner of the room, silent, but attentive. Both types of observation require a careful planning structure.

Structuring observations

The nature and purpose of the observation process will influence the level of structuring we need to introduce. Through structured observations, we can gather both qualitative and quantitative data. Using carefully designed checklists or observation schedules, we can record behaviour patterns and the number of actions and interactions. In semi-structured observation procedures one may still use checklists and schedules, but some flexibility is required to record both comments and unexpected outcomes. In action research, I feel that the flexibility of recording unexpected outcomes is of some value.

Contexts for observation

Let us now consider some contexts in which an action researcher may make use of observation as a method of data-gathering.

Observing colleagues

If your project involves observing colleagues you need to have some dialogue with them to discuss both organisational issues and the principles you would want to follow during the observations. For example, you need to make decisions about where, how often and how long the observations will be. You will need to study any schedules and checklists and establish a common understanding of what you are observing. It is also advisable to discuss how you will share your observations with the observed and what form of feedback will be given. This kind of discussion will help to build up trust and make the whole process more effective. An example of this would be when you decide to research the teaching styles of a group of teachers. A researcher completing checklists and making notes would observe each of the colleagues. In this context you would have established, prior to the observation, what you are observing and recording and how you would validate your observations. When you are observing colleagues, consideration should also be given to your approach. You need to show sensitivity and be unobtrusive. Any feedback should be non-judgemental and relate to the criteria established between you and the observed.

The three-phase observation cycle proposed by Hopkins (2002) shown in Figure 5.1 is worthy of consideration.

Figure 5.1 **The three-phase observation cycle.**

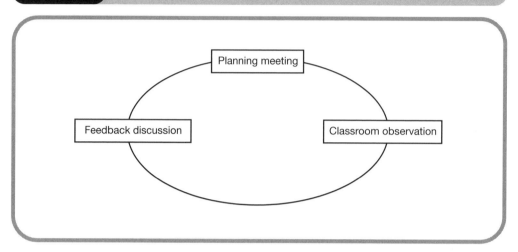

There are three essential phases in Hopkins's model. The *planning meeting* provides the observer and the teacher with an opportunity to reflect on a proposed lesson which then leads to a mutual decision to collect observational data on an aspect of the teacher's own practice. During the *classroom observation* phase, the observer observes the teacher in the classroom and collects objective data on an aspect of teaching they agreed upon earlier. During the *feedback session* the observer and the teacher share the information gathered during the observation, decide on appropriate action, agree a record of the discussion and then plan another round of observation.

Here is an example of an observation of a colleague by another colleague. The project title of the action research project was 'Who does the talking?' The project involved two teachers who decided to observe each other to establish the level of teacher talk in the classroom. The objective was to try to increase student participation and discussion and the starting point for this was to make an assessment of one's teaching style at the start of the project. Helen and Matthew, two colleagues, had an initial meeting to select a lesson for observation and studied the lesson plans. They decided that Helen would sit at the back of the classroom and make notes on the amount of time Matthew spent talking to the students and the length of time his pupils were involved in responding and discussing. She would also make a note of the nature of the questions he asked as they both felt that to be relevant. Helen drew a plan of the classroom and seating arrangements as they felt these too may have some impact on the level of pupils' involvement in the lesson. It was decided that Matthew would explain to his class that Helen was observing him in connection with her own studies, as he felt that being told the objective of the observation may encourage students to change their behaviour for that session, defeating the purpose of the activity.

After a lesson was observed, Helen and Matthew met and discussed Helen's notes and perceptions. They also discussed the possibility that the nature of a question may partly affect pupils' talk. They decided to change the nature of some questions and planned another observation.

Here it can clearly be seen how the observation process fits well into the action research model, which involves selecting a topic, planning, collecting data, and taking action based on the findings.

Observing pupils

The process described above may not be suitable if you are observing pupils. It is not always possible to plan and discuss your ideas with pupils, especially if they are younger. Having said that, some of my students had to tell their pupils why they were writing things down when the pupils became curious and wanted to know why they were making notes about them. To reduce the disruption, children were told that their teachers were making notes to help them to think about how their teaching could be made better.

One example of student observation involved watching a group of pupils who were referred to as *disruptive* to identify patterns in their behaviour such as the context, the nature of the lesson and the teacher input during the times in which disruptive behaviour occurred. For this exercise Carole, an Early Years teacher, decided to involve a colleague to carry out an open-ended observation of selected children using no preconceived plans or checklists.

The notes of the observer on Nadia, 4 years and 6 months, looked like this.

9.0 Nadia sits down in the front of the carpet; she is completely still.

9.04 Teacher greets the students and asks them what they had been doing over the weekend. Nadia, with a few others, puts her hand up.

9.06 Teacher selects Nathan to tell the class what he had been doing during the weekend.

9.12 Nadia gets up and goes to the front of the class, sits down and holds the teacher's hand. She then gets up again and goes to the choosing corner.

9.13 Teacher asks Nadia to come back to the carpet, which she does not do.

9.15 Teacher says, 'Come and tell us what you have been doing over the weekend'.

9.19 Nadia runs back to the carpet and enthusiastically talks about her visit to see a donkey…

Guidelines

- Decide whether you are going to be a participant or non-participant observer. When you wish to observe while you are working with a group of children, it can be difficult to be a non-participant observer.

- Consider access and timescales for your observations.

- Quite often a structured observation schedule is useful; this may be an established structure or one that you design for the purpose in hand.

- If you are using a predetermined checklist, you may want to record unexpected outcomes which could be of significance within the context of your project.

- Think about your analysis while preparing your observation schedules. Remember you will need to analyse your data soon afterwards.

- Consider how you will validate your observations.

- Try a pilot observation and refine the process as necessary.

- Make a note of any difficulties you encounter; these may be of significance when you analyse your data and write up your report.

Advantages of observation

- Open-ended observations allow you to capture all aspects of the topic of study.

- It offers first-hand data.

- It offers a way of studying, through close scrutiny of behaviour.

Disadvantages

- Too much information may be collected which could pose a challenge at the time of analysis.

- Organisational problems may stand in the way.

- Background noise and disruptions may lead to missing important data.

- There may be a temptation to miss out details if they do not fit the items on a checklist.

USING VIDEO RECORDINGS AND PHOTOGRAPHS

The use of videos to record events is becoming increasingly popular as a data-gathering technique. The availability of digital cameras and other technological resources has made video recording a viable and effective way of gathering information. One of the advantages of video recording is that it allows the researcher to observe an activity afterwards by watching the video, without the disruptions of the classroom or time constraints. By viewing recordings, practitioners can analyse different aspects of the activity as well as identify an unexpected point which may be significant. Video recordings are also very useful when it comes to collecting accurate information on student participation and attitudes. For recording critical incidents in the classroom a digital camera can provide both photographs and a few minutes of video recordings.

Advantages of video-recording

- Student behaviours and attitudes can be captured with greater accuracy than by making observation notes.

- Provides a permanent record of incidents, which can be viewed and reviewed.

- Makes sharing data with colleagues and fellow researchers easier to manage.

- Very useful at the time of dissemination. Recording provides powerful images which are hard to match through other means of communication.

- It makes it possible to carry out studies which need a sustained period of development and data collection so as to note changes.

- Video clips and films often generate a good deal of discussion.

Disadvantages

- Being recorded can be inhibiting and distracting for the participants.

- Those who are being recorded may behave differently in the presence of a camera.

- The usual technical hitches may lose useful first-hand data which cannot be replaced.

- Photographs may be selected according to the photographer's perception of the importance and significance of incidents.

An example of using video-recording for an action research project

Jill was carrying out an action research project on the impact of introducing a Critical Thinking programme to Year 8 students, in terms of raising student achievement and enhancing their level of confidence and listening skills. Jill chose a range of methods for collecting evidence for her project. She felt that she could track changes in students' achievement in terms of test scores and by collecting tangible examples of their work in a range of subjects over a period of time. She also felt that data on any possible changes in the level of students' participation in the programme, their confidence and listening skills were more effectively gathered through video recordings over a period of time.

Jill wrote in her report:

> My project was to explore whether the introduction of a structured Critical Thinking programme would help to raise my students' achievement in different subjects. Another objective of the study was to note any changes in students' confidence in taking part in discussions. I felt it was straightforward to compare the results using tests, but collecting evidence on changes in students' level of confidence and participation was rather more challenging. I needed something visual, which could be looked at over a period of time. Using video recordings provided me with an opportunity to achieve this. At the time of dissemination at the local teachers' centre, I showed sections of a video recording to illustrate students' behaviour over a period of six months. Data in the form of video recordings offered me authentic evidence to convince other people of the impact of my project.

QUALITY INDICATORS

Action research is a unique method for carrying out enquiries into aspects of practice. The purpose of action research makes it different from large-scale research studies. However, the action researcher still needs to consider questions of validity, reliability and generalisability within the context of their particular research study.

First, we need to consider the *validity* of the data. This means we need to consider the accuracy of what is collected and used as evidence. We should also be aware that the conclusions are based on the quality of what we gather as data. Interpretations of the same event or evidence can vary between different people. This can affect the validity of the data presented. One way of establishing validity, according to Mason (2002: 246) is to find 'various means of confirmation, such as arranging for a colleague to observe as well, arranging for audio or video recordings, and asking other participants for their versions'. Mason recommends triangulation for this purpose, which he describes as the process of obtaining several viewpoints or perspectives. The word 'triangulation', he explains, is based on the method of surveying land which breaks the region down into triangles, each of which is measured.

Hopkins (2002: 133) also emphasises the role of triangulation in data-gathering, 'as it involves contrasting perceptions of one actor in a specific situation against other actors in the same situation. By doing so, an initial subjective observation or perception is fleshed out and gives a degree of authenticity.' Hopkins quotes Elliot and Adelman (1976: 74) to describe the process of triangulation, which is useful for an action researcher to consider:

> Triangulation involves gathering accounts of a teaching situation from three quite different points of view; namely those of the teacher, his pupils and participant observer. Who in the 'triangle' gathers the accounts, how they are elicited, and who compares them, depends largely on the context.

The authors justify the process of gathering accounts from three distinct standpoints in terms of the three points of a triangle having a unique epistemological position.

In the context of action research we also need to consider the aspect of *reliability*. Reliability is described as: consistency or stability of a measure (Robson, 2002) and a consideration of whether, if the measure is repeated, one would obtain the same result. Hopkins (2002) makes a useful distinction of between validity, which reflects the internal consistency of one's research, and reliability, which reflects the generalisability of one's findings. He maintains that, in general, most action researchers and those who use qualitative methods are concerned with validity rather than reliability, in so far as their focus is a particular case rather than a sample.

In the case of practitioner research, the researcher needs to emphasise that generalisability is still possible, in terms of the project being applicable to other similar situations and, in some cases, the study's replicability.

CASE STUDIES

Many action research projects are written up as case studies. The following advantages of a case study outlined by Adelman *et al.* (1976) support the use of case studies as a means of disseminating action research projects. The authors' description of case studies demonstrates why they are a powerful means of capturing real data which can act as a basis for action.

- The data within a case study are strong in reality but susceptible to ready organisation. This strength in reality arises because case studies are down to earth and hold the attention, in harmony with the reader's own experience, and provide a natural basis for generalisation.

- Case studies are a 'step to action'. They begin in a world of action and contribute to it. Their insights may be directly interpreted and put to use for staff or individual self-development, for feedback within the institution, for formative evaluation, and for education policy-making.

SUMMARY

This chapter directs the reader's attention to issues of data collection. Large amounts of data, like literature, can be overwhelming in their abundance. Guidance on selection and pertinence has been given and a distinction was made between quantitative and qualitative data. The merits of qualitative data for the purpose of action research was highlighted. The importance of addressing ethical issues was also stressed. Issues of validity, reliability and generalisability, within the context of action research, were discussed and the role of triangulation as a means of quality control was also raised. The advantage of using case study as a method for disseminating action research was also briefly addressed.

Chapter 6

Analysing data

KEY POINTS

This chapter focuses on:

- sifting through data;
- ways of analysing and representing data;
- examples of data analysis.

INTRODUCTION

Your action research project is now entering a crucial stage. You have planned your project with meticulous attention and gathered data using different methods. Now it is time to do the final analysis and represent your data prior to drawing conclusions and implementing appropriate action. If you are engaged in a small-scale action research project with recurring cycles of planning – data-gathering – evaluating – acting, you will have been continually analysing your data and the final stage will be a pulling together of your findings. For a researcher who is undertaking a study which leads to a dissertation, the analysis stage involves taking a close look at all the data collected before presenting conclusions. Many of my students experience mixed feelings at the analysis stage. After many months of work, they feel quite excited about analysing the data before making conclusions as it marks a significant stage in their research process. They also often feel quite overwhelmed by the amount of data they have collected and feel a little unsure about how to get started with data analysis. I think if you have collected your data carefully and addressed the issues of validity and reliability, the analysis stage should not pose any real difficulties.

As an action researcher, you have to create a coherent story from all the data collected. It is likely that you have used qualitative methods for data collection and so the presentation of evidence mainly takes the form of descriptions. I personally feel that analysing qualitative data is equally as challenging as analysing and presenting quantitative evidence from large samples using statistical methods. At this point, the action researcher also needs to be aware of some of the criticisms made, by many, that action research is a 'soft' option in which the practitioner researcher works with a small number of people and therefore is not proper research. To address this criticism, I would just reiterate what I have said previously that an action researcher is involved in investigating a question or a topic within his or her own context where the focus is on a single case or a small group of people. It is part of the professional development of those involved. An action researcher is looking to create meanings using rich descriptions and narratives. The action researcher develops expertise through looking at situations closely and analysing them, recognising possible bias and interpreting data, rather than looking to generalise findings based on a study of large numbers of cases.

MAKING A START WITH ANALYSING DATA

Before starting to analyse files full of data, it is important for the action researcher to revisit the aims and expectations of the project. Think about what your research question or hypothesis was and remind yourself what it is that you have been investigating. This is always a good start. During data analysis you are trying to identify themes and patterns in order to be able to present robust evidence for any claims you make. You need to look at the data you have collected from several sources and relate them to what your original, expected outcomes were. Of course, as any good researcher, you would also be looking out for unexpected outcomes which may be of significance and report them too. Your conclusions must relate to the original aims and objectives. It is also useful to remind yourselves of your readings, which will certainly help in your analysis.

WAYS OF REPRESENTING DATA

There are many different ways in which you can analyse and present your data. You may also use a combination of the representations from the various models I discuss below.

Quantifiable data

The way you represent your data may depend on the type of data you have collected. An action researcher may have collected data which is quantifiable. For example, if your data collection involved questionnaires or quantifiable information through observations, that data can be displayed using tables and diagrams.

Including charts and diagrams is helpful in two different ways. First, a visual display makes it easier for the reader to understand information. Secondly, they break up continuous prose which can sometimes be tedious for a reader trying to make sense of the data. In a research project which explored the type of questions asked in a classroom, the researcher may present the information as a frequency table which is easy to understand. This type of information can also be presented in graphical form. When data is displayed in a graphical form, it is important to remember not to emphasise the findings in percentage terms as you are only studying small numbers. Making claims in percentage terms does not make much impact when you are only referring to a total number of ten or twenty.

Descriptive data

There are times when your descriptive data can be powerfully presented as profiles of students and in the form of diary entries of the researcher. During the analysis of data one action researcher, who carried out an intervention project to enhance the aspirations of pupils in an inner-city school, used student profiles and her own diary entries to create an authentic story of what had happened. Below are extracts from two examples of data presented by Alison for two of her students – Sara and Shaun.

Sara

Sara is 12 years old. Her results in Mathematics and Science at the end of Primary school were very good, but her English results were below average. Her communication skills were poor and, perhaps as a result, she hardly participated in class discussions. She was also reluctant to talk to her peers in small groups. During a parents' meeting, I found out that Sara's parents did not speak English and felt unable to support her with school work. During a discussion with her parents, with Sara present (as the translator), they informed me that they had no great hopes for Sara's future because she did not come from the right background for higher education ...

Researcher's diary

Today, I actually saw Sara talking to her friends and laughing during group work. It was two weeks ago that I nominated her and two of her friends to attend a drama club after school. Is the club attendance making a difference to her confidence in talking to others? A casual remark from her English teacher also suggested that her communication skills may be improving.

Shaun

Shaun is a bright boy of 12, although his ability is not manifested through traditional means. He hardly completes his class work and, as a result, it is difficult to assess his full potential. My gut feeling is that he is intellectually very capable. I have some evidence of this from observing him during a technology lesson where he created a stunning structure using straws and pins. I was not sure whether to include him in the group in my 'aspirations' project, but I did.

Researcher's diary

My notes today confirmed my hunch about Shaun. I overheard him talking to two boys, discussing a fee for doing their homework for them. When I subtly investigated this further, I found out that Shaun had been doing homework for other students and, in most cases, the work demonstrated the use of very sophisticated concepts and strategies.

Alison used the above entries to highlight an aspect that emerged during her analysis – that of unrealised potential – and how this may inhibit aspirations and achievement.

Data from interviews

Using interviews is a common method of data collection for action researchers. You may want to transcribe the whole of each interview or listen to the tape at the time of data analysis and use parts of the tape recordings as evidence where relevant. I recommend to my students that they include full transcripts in the appendix and use only extracts as pieces of evidence within the text. In the aspirations project I referred to above, a powerful piece of evidence Alison used in her report was the following extract from her interview with Shaun:

Shaun: I was afraid of that.

Alison: Afraid of what, Shaun?

Shaun: That you will push me into attending an after-school club. I think it is a waste of my valuable time.

Alison: Can you explain it to me? I am trying to figure out what you just said. What do you mean by waste of time?

Shaun: I don't want to join any clubs. I would rather stay at home and do something else. That is why I try not to do well in the tests, so that you won't include me in the bright kids group.

Presenting observations

As in the case of interviews, extracts from written observation notes can be used when presenting findings. Any other significant issues emerging from observations can also be included in an appendix so that the reader can refer to it if necessary or if interested.

A number of action researchers write up their projects in the form of case studies. Presenting data as a case study is particularly useful when the researcher employs observation as the main means of data collection. It is easier to record changes in the attitudes and behaviours of a small group of children in the form of a case study. As I mentioned in Chapter 5, case studies can bring a phenomenon to life and present the outcomes of research very powerfully.

Presentation of video recordings

Although video recordings provide a unique opportunity to gather real and authentic data as events occur, when it comes to presenting the data it poses a problem. The best possible way of conveying the richness of the data gathered through video recording is by making detailed notes about what has been recorded. Converting significant events into photographs will be one way of capturing at least the essence of what happened in a session.

THE PROCESS OF QUALITATIVE DATA ANALYSIS

As I discussed briefly in the previous chapter, qualitative data have some particular strengths for the action researcher. In a very illuminating text-book focusing on qualitative data analysis, Miles and Huberman (1994: 10) indicate the features of qualitative data which contribute to its strength 'as its focus on naturally occurring, ordinary events in natural settings, so that we have a strong handle on what "real life" is like'. The authors describe the quality of its 'local groundness', as the data is col-lected in close proximity to a specific situation. What also makes qualitative data very suitable for the action researcher, according to the authors, is its ability to capture the 'richness' and 'holism' of a situation.

For analysing and interpreting qualitative data, Miles and Huberman (1994) suggest a model which should guide you in your efforts to both make sense of the data and to share your interpretations with an audi-ence. They define data analysis as consisting of three concurrent flows of activity: *data reduction*, *data display* and *conclusion drawing/verification*. I have attempted, in the following sections, to explore these three processes in the context of an action researcher's efforts to analyse data. This three-component model also provides a useful framework for analysing data collected over a period of time.

Data reduction

Data reduction refers to the process of selecting, focusing, simplifying, abstracting and transforming the data that appear in the written up field notes or transcriptions. The action researcher is continually engaged in data reduction throughout the enquiry until the conclusions are presented. The authors describe data reduction as a form of analysis that sharpens, sorts, focuses, discards and organises data in such a way that 'final conclusions' can be drawn and verified. The data which emerge after this process is what you would use in your final analysis. For an action researcher, this continuous analysis and selection of relevant data is consistent with the emerging nature of participatory research.

Data display

Data displays can include different types of graphs, charts and networks. The purpose is to make organised information into an immediately available, accessible, compact form so that the analyst can see what is happening and either draw conclusions or move on to the next step of analysis which the display suggests to be useful.

Conclusion drawing and verification

From the start, the researcher tries to decide what things mean and to note regularities, patterns and explanations. The researcher holds these conclusions lightly, maintaining scepticism until they are more explicit and grounded. Although final conclusions appear only when the analysis is over, the action researcher also draws conclusions as the project progresses.

HOW DO I PRESENT THE EMERGING THEMES AND PATTERNS?

In Chapter 7, I have discussed in some detail how to report data. In this section my aim is to guide the reader through the presentation of analysed data. Again, let me remind you about the distinction between analysing and reporting an action research project as it progresses and a larger study, possibly one which leads to writing a formal dissertation. These are not watertight categories because quite often the categories and processes merge. In both types of situation what the researcher needs, as Strauss and Corbin (1998) state, is the ability to step back and critically analyse situations, to recognise and avoid bias to obtain valid and reliable data and to think abstractly. The process of analysis can then lead to theory building. One of the unique features of action research is that it provides opportunities for the researcher to construct personal theories based on evidence.

Here is an example of an action researcher who recently completed a small-scale project with me. Joanne's aim for the project was to encourage her Year 4 pupils to engage in more discussion. During the three months of her introducing practical activities using different stimuli, equipment and other resources, she kept a range of data such as: a log of what was happening in each of the practical sessions, tape recordings of children's discussions and observations by one of her colleagues of three lessons at different points during the project. Joanne analysed her data as she collected them and shared them with a critical friend. She wrote up her findings as a series of entries as the project progressed. In each of her entries she highlighted any changes in the children's attitudes to the tasks, the amount of talk in the sessions and her interpretation of the nature of their understanding of taught concepts. At the time of writing up her final report, Joanne drew her conclusions based on the analysis of her ongoing entries. The result was a personalised account of her experiences which led to her constructing a list of successful strategies used during her interventions, which she presented at a staff meeting. Joanne also presented a list of what she felt did not work so effectively. Her presentation was in the form of an ongoing story, which she felt was beneficial for herself as a researcher as well as making it accessible to the people she shared her findings with.

If you are engaged in a longer project, you may still want to follow the model I have just described, where you are analysing your data as the project progresses. Or you may decide to wait until you have collected the different types of data and then look for themes and patterns that emerge. In the latter case, I recommend the use of highlighter pens to mark sections of the data which suggest a particular theme or issue. When this kind of analysis is done the researcher should be able to present the findings under themes and draw on evidence from different sources of data to support any claims made. For example, there may be evidence from questionnaires and observational data to suggest the emergence of a particular theme. A video recording may add to the strength of your data. If some evidence emerges which does not support your findings, you should still present it and speculate and discuss possible reasons for this. At the time of analysing for themes and patterns, it is often useful to remind yourself of what your literature review highlighted with reference to those particular aspects. This will be of use at the time of writing a report.

EXAMPLES OF DATA ANALYSIS IN ACTION RESEARCH PROJECTS

Enhancing discussion skills in a Key Stage 1 classroom

Susannah, a class teacher of a group of 6-year-olds and who works in the same school as Joanne referred to in the previous section, set up an action research project which aimed to enhance the discussion skills of her children. After reading round the topic and seeking external advice and support on how to carry out her study, she set out her data-gathering process as follows:

- Pre- and post-project questionnaires with the whole class of 23 children. Questions were read to the children to avoid difficulties with reading distorting the data.

- Observation notes of lessons, every week, by the class teacher and a total of three observations by a colleague.

Before presenting her analysis of data, Susannah wrote the following:

> At the outset, I need to explain the difficulties I experienced in observing children. Being a participant observer created difficulties with observation. My presence during group work made the students talk less as they seemed to expect me to want them to work quietly. The data collected by my colleague as a non-participant observer provided more useful data.

The data were analysed in the following ways:

i. For both pre- and post-project questionnaires, students' perceptions of 'talking' in class were listed under different categories related to the questions asked. *Examples of questions analysed were*:

    – When do you talk in lessons?

    – When is talking in class useful?

    – Does talking make work easier or harder?

    – What does your teacher think of you talking in lessons?

ii. Detailed notes of lesson observations were given in the form of a narrative. Here is an extract:

> There were 5 children doing the activity – 3 boys and 2 girls. The activity was about guessing the mystery number from clues written on a card. 'Just one card with questions for all of us to share', muttered Ben. Asha looked disinterested and then looked in the direction of Melanie who was chatting away to everyone else, as she does during most of the activities. James and Stuart were talking from the start, but they were talking about a television programme and trying to work as a pair. Children were told that they could work together to find the answers to the mystery number questions. I was sitting nearby, but not participating. I had told the children they were not to come to me during this session because I was writing some notes for something I was doing for my own study. I observed the following:
>
> - Melanie talked the most and directed all the discussions about strategies. Ben tried to work with Melanie but did not get much of a chance to say much. Asha was quiet, as always, but was paying attention. Two of the other boys, James and Stuart, started working as a pair.

Susannah's analysis of the observation data in this example read as follows:

> It seemed that my expectation that one card with the questions will be sufficient for all 5 children was wrong. Ben articulated his concern straight away. Was I right in splitting Asha and Suresh, who usually work together, just for this experiment? James and Stuart choosing to work as a pair, within the group, suggests to me that five was too large a number for that particular activity …

In a subsequent observation Susannah tried a similar activity with four children and found that there was more interaction in that lesson. In her analysis of the observations she presented descriptions of what occurred in each of the group sessions and how her own strategies for grouping strategies changed the frequency and nature of the children's discussions.

An intervention programme to increase children's understanding of place value

Valerie, a Year 4 teacher, was undertaking a project for her Master's dissertation. She felt that an enhanced understanding of the principle that our number system is based on the value of a figure being determined by the position it occupies within a number is central to children's number work, so that an increased understanding of this principle would reduce their mistakes and help their mental arithmetic work.

Valerie's project aimed to set up an intervention programme which was designed to help her class of 30 children acquire a greater understanding of the place-value concept.

During the project, Valerie collected the following types of data:

- a pre- and post-test on mental arithmetic questions and written number operations, with the whole class;

- interviews with a smaller number of children, at pre- and post-project stages, asking them probing questions about their strategies and the reasons for any errors they had made;

- observation notes of children working with a set of activities and tape-recording of their conversations over a period of eight weeks.

In her data analysis, Valerie presented

- the pre-and post-test results in the form of a graph, which clearly indicated the changes in children's scores, showing if and how responses to particular questions improved or not;

- an analysis of different strategies and the reasons for children's errors using evidence provided pre- and post-project by interview transcripts;

- a list of significant issues which emerged during the intervention programmes, outlining ongoing changes of strategies.

Valerie reported her findings under different themes, drawing on the different types of data she had analysed.

⬤ Introducing Critical Thinking – a case study

As part of a project funded by the local education authority, Adrian's project was to introduce a Critical Thinking course to Year 8 students. He had a list containing a set of objectives for the project. He decided to use video recordings as his main data collection method. He recorded a lesson each week and wrote a commentary every time. His intention was to analyse his notes on the basis of the objectives for the project and to refine his lessons on the basis of the emerging analysis. The first video recording showed Adrian interrupting the students too much. In his notes he made the comment that the constant interruptions did not give the students much opportunity for independent thinking, to exercise metacognitive skills as he described it, which was one of the objectives of the Critical Thinking course. Adrian realised this and, as his action plan for the next lesson, he decided to tell the students that he would be talking less when they were working on their tasks, but was happy to be asked for support and help when it was needed. He also assured them that he would be happy to listen to any individual or group who may wish to share their ideas with him at any time. In the second video taped lesson, Adrian noticed that his interruptions were less and that the students stayed on task for longer. They also took more initiative and generated new ideas. However, he was concerned that his input was too restricted and wanted to take a more active part during children's discussions. Adrian asked a colleague to observe a third video taped lesson and to discuss ways forward. He also found some literature on Critical Thinking which gave him more insights into the objectives for the Critical Thinking lessons, such as encouraging processes of reasoning, seeking evidence and critically appraising one's beliefs. With an increased understanding of aspects of Critical Thinking and more support from his colleague, Adrian planned the next two lessons. A new strategy for the next lesson involved Adrian working with small groups asking them questions which specifically encouraged them to use Critical Thinking skills. The new strategy worked well, except that some of the other groups were disruptive and did not engage in the tasks while Adrian was working with a small group. He changed his teaching strategy again and decided to provide each group with a set of questions to consider while they were working on a task, as he circulated between groups. This strategy seemed to work better.

Adrian's analysis for his action research project took the form of dated diary entries of how he saw his own teaching of Critical Thinking, based on the video recordings and notes of his discussions with his colleague. Each diary entry was analysed and a list of significant events and changes were listed. Adrian's final report charted his journey through the project and he discussed his own professional development through his experiences; this formed the basis of a national conference presentation he made.

SUMMARY

This chapter focused on data analysis which precedes writing up a report. Various forms of data summaries were presented. The extraction of themes and patterns emerging from the collected data is recommended. Video recordings were referred to as a mixed blessing for the researcher, visual evidence being an accurate, unedited portrayal of what occurred, but there are potential difficulties with their transcription into descriptions. Finally, a synopsis of three case studies was provided as I believe that aspects of data analysis may be better understood within the reality of actual action research projects.

Chapter 7

Writing up and reporting your action research

KEY POINTS

This chapter looks at:

- the process of writing up action research;
- the structure of a dissertation;
- the use of case study for presenting action research.

INTRODUCTION

I will start this chapter with a quotation from one of my Master's student's work which catches the spirit of what I want to say in this chapter. Ann wrote:

> For me writing a report of my action research was a very special time. It was like telling someone the story of my professional journey. It was a time for further reflection on what I had learnt and understood and also about forming a vision of other horizons. The process of writing an account of what and how I did my research brought it all together to me and it was very rewarding. Writing the final report made me realise that I have emerged from the experience of action research feeling more confident and enlightened. Not only that I found out much more about aspects of my practice and

new directions to take, I also realised that I have become more curious and ask more questions … (Ann, Key Stage 2 teacher)

Ann, like many other teacher-researchers, carried out an action research
project on a topic which arose from her intrinsic motivation to improve
her practice. She was expected to write up a report for her school and
she found the whole process rewarding. In some cases an action
researcher engaging in activities for the purpose of improving practice
may not be required to produce a written report. But for those who are
in the process of writing a final report of their action research, useful
guidance is provided by Hopkins (2002: 140) who feels that all action
researchers need to put their data together in such a way that:

- the research could be replicated on another occasion;

- the evidence used to generate hypotheses and consequent action is
  clearly documented;

- action taken as a result of the research is monitored;

- the reader finds the research accessible and it resonates with his or
  her own experience.

At this point, I reflect on my own experiences in my role of supporting
action researchers in a variety of contexts. For example, you may have
been carrying out your study for several months or years depending on
your circumstances and it is time to write a report on your study for the
purpose of obtaining a qualification. Or it may be that you have carried
out action research and it is time to disseminate your findings in some
way. This could take the form of a written report or some other form of
presentation. First I will deal with written reports and then, later in the
chapter, share some examples of presentations of action research that I
have had the privilege to attend.

WRITING A REPORT ON YOUR ACTION RESEARCH

Whether you are writing a report as part of the requirement of an
accredited course or for the purpose of just making it available for
others to read, here are some factors to consider. Remind yourself that
the mode of study that you have selected is action research and the pur-

pose of action research is to improve practice or to implement change for the purpose of professional development. The intention of the action researcher is not to make generalisable claims, but to tell a story which is of interest to other practitioners who may want to learn from it, or replicate the study or apply your findings to their situations.

What kind of report?

From the outset, it is important to consider the audience, the requirements and the purpose of your report.

Audience

First the audience. Ask yourself: who is my audience? You may have obtained funding from an external source for your action research and, in such cases, you may have been given a specific format to follow. The case studies of teacher-researchers reporting their findings, funded by the Teacher Training Agency in 1997, all started with the following four common subheadings and then the writers selected headings which were appropriate for the work they were reporting.

- Aims

- Dimensions of the case study

- Summary of findings of the case study

- Background.

It may be that you are writing a report or dissertation as part of the requirement for a qualification. In this case, your dissertation will be read by academic tutors and sometimes by an external examiner. If this is the purpose of your report you will be expected to follow a particular format and the conventions of scholarship. In a long study or a dissertation you will also be expected to show some knowledge of recent and relevant research literature. Whatever the purpose of your report, it is important to be clear and consistent and demonstrate a good understanding of the issues you are researching. In the case of a dissertation for accreditation purposes, the expectation will be that the study is extensive as you would be considering yourself an expert in your chosen area of study. While reporting an action research, the quality of your writing can be enhanced by writing in an authentic and personal style. I have always felt that reporting action research is often powerful for one's own professional development because of the personal nature of the writing. It is helpful to remember that you are reporting your own story that you have constructed from your experiences and collaborations with other people.

Think of the reader

A useful strategy to adopt when writing your report is to consider the potential readers of your report. The following guidance may be of help:

- Always provide the background of the study and the context of the action researcher. This helps the reader to relate to your report and possibly apply the findings to their own circumstances.

- It is important to present your aims at the outset and present your findings within the context of what you have set out to achieve.

- Readers appreciate realism and honesty. It makes sense to report what has progressed magnificently as well as any difficulties you may have experienced.

- Present your plans and outlines of action clearly. It is possible that others may want to replicate what you did or report your findings to their colleagues.

- As action research is often a personal journey, writing the report in the first person is more effective. Sentences such as 'I chose this method because I had the opportunity to study this as part of our school-based professional development...' or 'I changed direction after finding out...' makes the text reader-friendly and more accessible.

- Don't assume that readers always know what you are discussing. Try and explain items in simple, clear language. Keep the target audience in mind. If your report is going to be read by parents and governors, it would be inadvisable to use education jargon which you may effectively have used to disseminate information to your colleagues.

- Use subheadings where possible. It is easier to read text with subheadings.

- Be creative in your presentation. This is possible within any given format. Some of my students use bubbles, cartoons and photographs containing evidence when they present their findings.

WRITING A DISSERTATION

In this section I will try to provide some guidance on writing a dissertation based on your action research. It is not, by any means, meant to be a definitive document. I don't believe that a fixed set of rules can ever be applicable when you write up action research, because at the very heart of an action research project is the opportunity to be flexible, emergent and creative. However, if you are writing a dissertation for accreditation purposes, you need to follow the format given by the institution. Within that set format, there is still plenty of opportunity to be original.

A dissertation is the culmination of the work you have undertaken which should demonstrate to your reader your personal understanding of an issue, what action you have taken and how these actions have informed and developed your professional life. The emphasis is on personal learning and not in providing generalisations about education.

As your study is likely to be an enquiry into your own practice you need to pay attention to the following:

- Acknowledge your own beliefs, prior assumptions and values within the report, at the start.

- You need to acknowledge your inevitable subjectivity, upfront.

- Say, at the outset, that the interpretations are personal and that others may interpret your data differently.

- State clearly what methods were used for data-gathering and how multiple perspectives were sought.

- Discuss ethical issues and how they have been addressed.

Maintaining quality·

If you have a set of criteria for grading your dissertation, you must read them first. The following general guidance should help to monitor the quality of your work. You must:

- make your aims and objectives clear;

- justify why you are undertaking the work – provide a rationale;

- acknowledge your own perspectives and beliefs;

- make the context clear – this is important as action research, in most cases, is located within a distinct situation of the practitioner;

- demonstrate your understanding of issues;

- show that you have made efforts to read work carried out by others in your area of research and any theoretical literature relating to your study;

- show how you collected data and how you have made efforts to triangulate the information;

- present the data in an accessible manner and in such a way that the reader can identify the evidence for your conclusions;

- make coherent arguments;

- demonstrate your personal learning.

All dissertations should have the following features:

- clear formulation of the research question or topic of study;

- a critical account of theories and research, including your own viewpoints and commentary;

- justified methods of enquiry;

- clearly presented data;

- robust analysis of data;

- discussion of findings and emerging issues;

- reflection on both your findings and the methodology used;

- limitations;

- enhancement of personal knowledge;

- reflection on personal action and future directions;

- an organised bibliography.

Structuring a dissertation

As mentioned previously, higher education institutions usually provide a basic format for writing a disserfation. A close study of the formats issued by a few institutions showed that although there were differences in the words used to describe the different parts of a dissertation, they all seemed to require similar content. In the following section, I will present a set of guidelines that I provide my students. They are in the form of chapter headings for writing a dissertation (with approximately 15,000 words in total). These guidance notes may be adapted for all courses leading to a qualification. Remember, I am referring to the format of a dissertation which arises from carrying out an action research project.

Abstract

This section will provide a short summary of the aims, methodology, findings and implications for practice. This must be a *brief* section – about 200 words should be sufficient. I ask my students to complete it on two sides of a postcard and show it to me before they write the abstract. Many of my students finalise their abstract after writing the rest of the dissertation – this is wise because during the writing up process your thoughts come together and help you to present an effective abstract. Do remember that the abstract is the first section of your study read by your supervisor or examiner and first impressions are important. Don't forget your study may be placed in the library where others who are interested may read it. It is customary to use the past tense here, as you are reporting what has already been done.

Table of contents

Chapter 1 – Introduction

In this chapter the writer sets the context of the study and discusses the reasons for undertaking the study. What was the personal motivation? Why at this time? What are the trends in the topic of study in terms of recent local, national or international developments, using some references to the literature? What specific aspect of the topic do you intend to study? If it is a research question, or hypothesis, present it clearly. New initiatives? What are your aims? This chapter also provides a guide, as signposts, for the reader about what to expect in each chapter; this needs to be in a short summarised form.

(About 1,500 words)

Chapter 2 – Review the literature

This chapter should present the reader with a comprehensive review of the literature relating to your topic of study. References are made to recent and relevant literature – theory and research – on your topic. Are there any current debates on your choice of topic? What has been written about the topic and who wrote it? I often ask my students to present the literature in themes. The ideas you have gathered from your literature search should be analysed. The purpose of this chapter is to locate your study within a framework informed by what is out there and what has already been found out. This is, therefore, an important chapter which needs careful planning and organisation. Rather than listing each writer's views or theories, try to connect different perspectives of different authors by drawing on similarities and contrasts in their thinking. Presenting a summary of what each author has said without pulling the ideas together makes tedious reading. Use subheadings where you can and make a brief critical commentary of your own on what is being presented.

(About 3,000 words)

Chapter 3 – Methodology

In your dissertation you would acknowledge action research as your mode of study. Why did you choose action research? Here you need to discuss the features of action research which make it suitable for your study. What is action research? Discuss very briefly how action research evolved, over the years, as a method of enquiry for practitioners. What models of action research do you know about and what is your understanding of these models? What are the advantages of action research as a method? Relate these specifically to your project. Show the reader that you are also aware of the limitations of action research and respond to these in terms of the study you are about to embark on. You should describe the design of the study and the preparations and planning that preceded action. How did you collect the data? Did you use observations? Interviews? Videos?

Diaries? Why did you select the methods? Justify your choices and also show that you are aware of the limitations of each method you used. Ethical considerations should be included in this chapter.
(About 2,500 words)

Chapter 4 – Action and data collection

For this chapter you may use a different title such as 'Activities', 'What did I do?' or 'Implementing action' or 'gathering data', or any other phrase which you feel most appropriately reflects what you did for your project. In this chapter you must give sufficient detail for others to understand what you have done. Bear in mind that others may want to replicate your project. Explain your data-gathering methods, your first trials and report any modifications you had to make. This chapter would contain detailed narratives of what you did, highlighting outcomes using a range of techniques. Transcripts of tape recordings, observation notes and references to photographs can be used to provide evidence for any claims you may make later. Your aim is to present a detailed and effective account of what happened during the action stage and to present your findings. If you revised your action, you may want to refer to the succession of action cycles within your action research. Don't forget to justify how you addressed the issues of validity and reliability. Who did you share your data with? Did you use critical friends or colleagues to achieve triangulation of your data?
(About 3,000–4,000 words)

Chapter 5 – Analysis of data and results

What did you find out? Include evidence to back up your claims. Extracts from tape recordings, observations and personal logs may be used. Documentary evidence can also be presented. What has changed? Your claims must always be supported by robust data. You may find it useful to follow the guidelines provided in Chapter 6 of this book. The findings you present in this chapter must inform the reader of the impact your project has made.
(About 2,500 words)

Chapter 6 – Conclusions and discussion

What are your conclusions? What themes have emerged from your study? How does it relate to your professional situation? Do your findings reflect what others have found out? Has your study generated evidence which contradicts the outcomes of studies carried out by others? In this chapter, you need to give an account of your own personal learning. Reflect on the outcomes of the project. What personal theories can you make on the basis of your study? How will your findings influence your practice? What are the implications of your research for you and for others? Were there any parts of the study which posed problems? What do you think of your methods of data collection? Were they suitable? List and discuss any limitations of your study. What future direction does the study suggest?

(About 3,000 words)

Bibliography

Appendices

⬤ Test your understanding of report structure

Below is an exercise for you which should help you to internalise the structure of a report.

The following extracts are taken from the MA dissertation of a student who obtained high marks from an external examiner, and was written using the above format. The title of the dissertation is: 'The role of speaking and writing in mathematics as a way of enhancing mathematical understanding'. The personalised and reflective nature of the writing was given special credit. (Note that full references were provided in the original dissertation but are not reproduced here.)

Try to write down the number of the chapter where you think each of the extracts appeared. For obvious reasons the chapter extracts are not in any special order. I have provided a list of the chapters where these appeared at the end of the section. I must remind you that this is an example of just one dissertation, and that this format may not be suitable for all reports. I hope it will still help you to think about the structure and style of writing of a dissertation or report.

A. My interest in the topic began when I listened to a lecture on the role of language in mathematics. I felt excited and wanted to find out more about it.

B. Here I acknowledge the inevitable subjectivity in interpreting the data. But I feel reassured by the fact that action research allows me to draw personal insights from this project. Any claims I make are only applicable to my study. However, others who read this report may be able to identify features which are applicable to them.

C. I found out that literature on mathematics communication is sparse, especially in the United Kingdom. I found Brissenden's (1986) argument that communication and discussion in mathematics are essential ingredients in promoting mathematics learning very convincing. His views are similar to what Vygotsky (1976) ... My own experience with Year 4 children has shown ...

D. Natalie, age 9, emphatically told me that you only write diaries in English lessons. The conversation I taped during a lesson with a group of four children provided evidence of their perception of mathematics as a discipline which is about numbers and doing sums. Here is an extract from Natalie's conversation with me.

Teacher: What I would like you to do is to keep a mathematics diary for the next few weeks, where I would like you to write down what you have learnt and what you think of a lesson.

Natalie: But, miss, we keep a diary for our news every week. Isn't diary writing for English lessons?

Teacher: What makes you think that a diary is only used for an English lesson?

Natalie: Because, mathematics is really all about numbers. We do sums in maths lessons. How can I write a diary in mathematics. There is nothing to write. You don't talk in mathematics. Do you?...

E. The key questions I wish to investigate are:

- Can more discussions in mathematics lessons enhance children's mathematical understanding of concepts?
- What changes may occur in terms of children's confidence and attitudes by introducing more talk and writing in mathematics lessons?

F. What I am still not sure of is how one can structure mathematical talk as part of the National Numeracy Strategy. The strategy does encourage discussion, but I am always aware of the timed three-part lesson which is at odds with a natural flow of unconstrained discussion. I will need to resolve this ...

G. Looking back at my study, I realise how my practice has changed in terms of making my questions more open-ended. An analysis of the type of questions I had asked the children showed that I didn't really give them many opportunities to talk, I was too passive myself ...

H. As part of my action research, I planned two types of intervention. This I will refer to as my first cycle of activities. Monitoring the effects of these interventions, I knew I would be able to plan other activities or modify my ideas.

I. One of the findings which emerged was the increased level of confidence demonstrated by the children. Their talk quite often reflected a higher level of learning. As I began to discuss more in their group time, they started using more sophisticated language and seemed to better understand the concepts relating to the words. What I discussed in Chapter 2 with reference to Vygotsky's (1978) Zone of Proximal Development highlighting the role of an adult scaffolding children in supporting their learning was in evidence ...

J. What have I learnt?

Changing my practice was a challenge. For years, my own perception of the nature of mathematics had been that it was a structured but lifeless discipline consisting of numbers, four rules of number and correct answers. I needed a lot of guidance before I could embark on this project. But the result was worth the effort. My perceptions have changed and this was brought about by watching my children grow in confidence. Both my children and I now 'speak' mathematics ...

K. My way forward is to share my ideas with my colleagues. I would feel that I have not really completed my story until I have told it to some more people and find out if they feel as excited about it as I do ...

L. The methods I used had to be appropriate for the context I am working in. I was a class teacher. I had an opportunity to undertake a project based in my classroom. I could collect information by listening and observing my children. I also had access to their written work which I could monitor over a period. Then I also needed an ongoing record of my experiences. I could clearly see what Carr and Kemmis (1986) meant by action research offering real opportunities for reflecting on practice based on evidence. I drew up an observation schedule and justified the value and advantages of this method of collecting data in real setting ...

Now that you have completed the task, I can tell you where in Deborah's dissertation the above extracts are from. I have reproduced more extracts from Chapter 6 as most researchers find this part of the writing more challenging.

A – Chapter 1
B – Chapter 3
C – Chapter 2

CREATIVE PRESENTATIONS OF ACTION RESEARCH

Here I draw on my experience of working with action researchers using creative ways of presenting their findings. Some practitioners presented their research findings to colleagues and others at conferences before writing their final reports as they believed that the preparation for the presentation helped to bring their thoughts together. Others presented their research outcomes after writing their reports. Some of the researchers did not actually write a formal report, but disseminated their research in other ways, which still served the purpose of bringing their ideas together and reflecting on them before sharing their work with others. So what forms of presentations are possible? Here are some examples of how you may present the outcomes of your action research, but for an imaginative practitioner there must be many other ways of designing an effective presentation.

Displays

Andrew, a Year 9 teacher, displayed the outcomes of his research on introducing Critical Thinking to his students, as an exhibition at the local teachers' centre. Titles of the different sections of his display were:

● *Main title*: Introducing Critical Thinking to students in Year 9

● *Subtitles*:

– What is Critical Thinking?

– Why use Critical Thinking with students?

- Critical Thinking in action

- What did the children say and do?

- What did I observe?

- High and low days

- What did my colleagues think?

- My thoughts on the influence of Critical Thinking on student learning

The exhibition gave Andrew plenty of opportunities to display his evidence and pose questions and include his own reflective commentary (in bubbles). With the rapid advancement of software packages these days it is possible to create impressive displays.

Conference presentations

Another way of disseminating action research is for the researchers to make presentations to interested audiences. Three examples of such presentations, arising out of projects I have guided, come to mind. One was a presentation of a project by a group of teachers, also guided by two LEA advisers from Kent, to explore ways in which talented young children's emotional needs could be met. The teacher-researchers shared their project at a national conference, with an audience of 120 early years practitioners. Using PowerPoint slides and clips of video recordings, the presenters brought the project to life. The story being told by class teachers, using powerful images, added to the interest in the project which led to many of the participants wanting them to share their experiences in their local venues.

The second presentation at a DfES conference – researching the possibility of introducing the well-known Italian early years 'Reggio Emelia' programme in Key Stage 1 classrooms in the UK – involved an academic at Exeter University working with a group of teachers. This too led to considerable interest among practitioners who either wished to participate in the project or replicate it in their local contexts.

The third presentation of a mathematics enrichment project was presented by two practitioners alongside a group of children who convincingly portrayed the impact of an intervention study on children's learning and attitudes. They used examples of video clips of work, transcripts of interviews and a series of *before* and *after* images of the improvement in their spoken and written work.

Telling a story as a case study

In recent times many case studies of action research are posted on websites (see the section on Useful websites at the end of the book). Within the interpretive and emergent methodology of action research, the process of writing case studies can often help the researcher to reconstruct a convincing story. These stories are often found more accessible to readers than research reports. Walker (1986: 189) describes a case study as a study of

> Particular incidents and events, and the selective collection of information on biography, personality, intentions and values [which] allows the case study worker to capture and portray those elements of a situation and give it meaning.

I feel that writing case studies is an ideal way of disseminating action research, as it can offer a meaningful story to the reader in a style suited for readers who are interested in the practical implications of an action research project.

SUMMARY

This chapter dealt with report writing which can often be the final stage for the action researcher. After the choice of topic, cycles of enquiry, data collection and analysis, the end is in sight. The report is the ultimate activity serving the purpose of portraying the action research as your attempt to investigate a phenomenon and disseminate your findings on which to base further practical changes. The target audience, its interest and disposition need to be borne in mind. A dissertation will have to conform to specified guidelines provided by an institution. A collection of extracts from a dissertation was given to help the reader to relate to the style and content of a dissertation. The possibility of disseminating action research findings as case studies, exhibitions and conferences was discussed.

Endnote

I wonder how many of the readers, first approaching this book, had a view of academic researchers as esoteric dwellers in ivory towers in which their output simply accumulated dust? I hope you now appreciate that action research methodology has been steered throughout its evolution by some talented academics responsible for conceptual instruments and the refinement of their use. The major ongoing value of action research is in the hands of readers such as yourself. Action research methodology in the hands of practitioner researchers has become the DIY of education research. I emphasise, however, that successful engagement requires the researcher to be **D**etermined, **I**ndustrious and **Y**earning for transformations.

Writing this book has been a pleasurable journey for me. It has offered me an opportunity to reflect on the benefits of practitioner research for both the individual and for their institutions. I wish you luck in your own action research.

Useful websites

The following websites are useful resources for an action researcher:

- www.bera.ac.uk – the British Educational Research Association website provides a list of ethical guidelines.

- www. standards.dfes.gov.uk/research – the DfES website provides summaries of the latest research and case studies.

- www.nfer.ac.uk – the National Foundation for Educational Research provides research summaries and reports of recent research projects.

- www.ncsl.org.uk – the National College of School Leadership website includes details of teachers using research.

- www.triangle.co.uk – *Action Research*, an academic journal which publishes studies of interest to action researchers.

- www.did.stu.mmu.ac.uk/carn – the Collaborative Action Research Network provides details of research publications and research conferences.

Glossary of key terms

Do you feel mystified by some terms in the research language? Here are some explanations. They are only meant as a start for you to investigate further as you proceed with your research.

Case study. A case study is an enquiry into a particular case or cases. You may seek data from multiple sources of evidence. The knowledge you generate relates to the case or cases you have selected, based on your understanding of the cases. Case studies often provide you with in-depth knowledge of situations.

Data. This is the information you collect as a researcher. You may generate a lot of it as tape-recorded interviews, questionnaires, field diaries and documentary evidence. It is very important that you design an effective, personal system to organise the data.

Data analysis. In general terms, this is the process of making interpretations of the data you have collected and possibly constructing theories based on your interpretations.

Documentary analysis. This relates to the process of analysing and interpreting data gathered through documents. For example, government documents, school policies, contents of meetings, diaries or school records are studied and analysed to make observations.

Emergent quality. In action research, the investigator makes adjustments to his or her plans in response to ongoing assessments. The cyclic nature of action research allows a researcher to take account of a quality which has emerged and which was not exhibited in the previous cycle.

Ethics. This is concerned with ethical principles and adherence to professional codes. These principles need to be at the centre of data-gathering, data analysis and writing up of projects.

Field notes and field diaries. These are entries made by researchers based on their observations and thoughts. Field notes do not have to be in written form; audio tapes and video tapes can be employed to gather authentic data. In participant observations, the use of field notes can be particularly useful.

Objectivity. It is a complex term, but in practice it involves the avoidance of any intrusion of a researcher's preconceptions or value judgements. Objectivity is a means of avoiding bias and prejudice in one's interpretations.

Participant observer. If, as a researcher, you are involved in what is being studied you are a participant observer. In action research you are likely to be involved in the project as a participant observer.

Qualitative/quantitative methods. The simplest explanation is to describe qualitative data as being in the form of descriptions using words, whereas quantitative data involve numbers. The debate as to which methods are more reliable goes on; I recommend that you select the methods which are likely to provide appropriate data for your purpose.

Reliability. You can describe a study as reliable if it can be replicated by another researcher. Careful documentation and clear articulation of procedures can contribute to greater reliability.

Subjectivity. The personal views and the commentaries of the researcher can sometimes be viewed as bias, but do not have to be so. If you declare the possible subjective nature of your statements or personal judgements and provide justifications for them these can be powerful in constructing arguments within action research.

Triangulation. Triangulation is recommended as a way of establishing the validity of findings. The researcher collects data from multiple sources involving multiple contexts, personnel and methods. The process of triangulation involves sharing and checking data with those involved. This should lead to the researchers being able to construct a more reliable picture.

Validity. In action research, validity is achieved by sound and robust data collection and the consensus of accurate interpretations. The latter is a contentious issue in my view as interpretations can be very personal in nature and achieving consensus may not always be possible within action research. Different interpretations of a situation may add to a debate and lead to personal and professional development of the researchers.

References

Adelman, C., Jenkins, D. and Kemmis, S. (1976) 'Rethinking Case Study: Notes from the Second Cambridge Conference', *Cambridge Journal of Education*, 6, 3: 139–50.

Bassey, M. (1998) 'Action Research for Improving Practice', in Halsall, R. (ed.), *Teacher Research and School Improvement: Opening Doors from the Inside*. Buckingham: Open University Press.

Bell, J. (1999) *Doing Your Research Project: A Guide for First-Time Researchers in Education and Social Science*. Buckingham: Open University Press.

Blaxter, L., Hughes, C. and Tight, M. (1996) *How to Research*. Buckingham: Open University Press.

Carr, W. and Kemmis, S. (1986) *Becoming Critical: Education, Knowledge and Action Research*. London: Falmer.

Chan, J. (2004) 'Take Control', *Times Educational Supplement*, 11 June.

Cohen, L. and Manion, L. (1994) *Research Methods in Education*. London: Routledge.

Department for Education and Employment (1999) *Excellence in Cities*. London: DfES.

Department for Education and Employment (2001) *Teaching and Learning: A Strategy for Professional Development*. London: DfEE.

Elliot, J. (1991) *Action Research for Educational Change*. Buckingham: Open University Press.

Elliot, J. and Adelman, C. (1976) *Innovation at Classroom Level: A Case Study of the Ford Teaching Project*, Open University Course E203: Curriculum Design and Development. Milton Keynes: Open University Educational Enterprises.

Hargreaves, D. (1996) *Teaching as a Research-Based Profession: Possibilities and Prospects*. Teacher Training Agency Annual Lecture, April.

Hopkins, D. (2002) *A Teacher's Guide to Classroom Research*. Buckingham: Open University Press.

Kemmis, K. and McTaggart, R. (2000) 'Participatory Action Research', in N. Denzin and Y. Lincoln. (eds.), *Handbook of Qualitative Research*. London: Sage.

Lewin, K. (1946) 'Action Research and Minority Problems', *Journal of Social Issues*, 2: 34–46.

MacGarvey, L. (2004) 'Becoming Marvellous', *Times Educational Supplement*, 11 June.

Macintyre, C. (2000) *The Art of Action Research in the Classroom*. London: David Fulton.

Mason, J. (2002) *Researching Your Own Practice: The Discipline of Noticing*. London: Routledge Falmer.

Miles, M. and Huberman, M. (1994) *Qualitative Data Analysis*. Beverly Hills, CA: Sage.

O'Leary, Z. (2004) *The Essential Guide to Doing Research*. London: Sage.

Reason, P. and Bradbury, H. (2001) *Handbook of Action Research: Participative Enquiry and Practice*. London: Sage.

Robson, C. (2002) *Real World Research*. Oxford: Blackwell.

Rose, R. (2002) 'Teaching as a "Research-based Profession": Encouraging Practitioner Research in Education', *British Journal for Special Education*, 29, 1: 44–8.

Schön, D. (1991) *The Reflective Practitioner*. New York: Basic Books.

Stenhouse, L. (1975) *An Introduction to Curriculum Research and Development*. London: Heinemann.

Stenhouse, L. (1983) *Authority, Education and Emancipation*. London: Heinemann.

Strauss, A. and Corbin, J. (1998) *Basic Qualitative Research*. London: Sage.

Teacher Training Agency (1998) *School-Based Research Consortia Initiative. Annual Review*. London: TTA.

Times Educational Supplement (2004) 'Classroom Discoveries', Special Edition, 11 June.

Vygotsky, L. (1978) *Mind in Society*. Cambridge, MA: Harvard University Press.

Walker, R. (1986) 'The Conduct of Educational Case Studies: Ethics, Theory and Procedures', in M. Hammersley (ed.), *Controversies in Classroom Research*. Milton Keynes: Open University Press.

Zeichner, K. (2001) 'Educational Action Research', in P. Reason and H. Bradbury (eds.), *Handbook of Action Research: Participative Enquiry and Practice*. London: Sage.

Index